TEACHER'S PET PUBLICATIONS

PUZZLE PACK
for
Dracula
based on the book by
Bram Stoker

Written by
Mary B. Collins

© 2006 Teacher's Pet Publications
All Rights Reserved

The materials in this packet are copyrighted
by Teacher's Pet Publications, Inc.

These pages may be duplicated by the purchaser
for use in the purchaser's own classroom.

Copying any of these materials and distributing them
for any other purpose is a violation of the copyright laws.

© 2006 Teacher's Pet Publications, Inc.
www.tpet.com

INTRODUCTION
If you already own the LitPlan for this title, this Puzzle Pack will refresh your Unit Resource Materials and Vocabulary Resource Materials sections plus give you additional materials you can substitute into the tests. If you do not already have a complete LitPlan, these pages will give you some supplemental materials to use with your own plan. There are two main groups of materials: one set for unit words (such as characters' names, symbols, places, etc.) and one set for vocabulary words associated with the book.

WORD LIST
There is a word list for both the unit words and the vocabulary words. These lists show you which words are being used in the materials and the clues or definitions being used for those words. You may want to give students a word list with clues/definitions to help them, or you may want students to only have a word list (without clues/definitions) if you want them to work a little harder. Both are available for duplication. The word lists can also be your "calling key" for the bingo games.

FILL IN THE BLANK AND MATCHING
There are 4 each of the fill in the blank and matching worksheets for both the unit and vocabulary words. These pages can be used either as extra worksheets for students or as objective parts of a unit test. They can be done individually if students need extra help or as a whole class activity to review the material covered.

MAGIC SQUARES
The magic squares not only reinforce the material covered but also work on reasoning and math skills. Many teachers have told us that their students really enjoy doing these!

WORD SEARCH PUZZLES
The word search words go in all directions, as indicated on your answer keys. Two of the word search puzzles have the clues listed rather than the words. This makes the puzzle a little more difficult, but it reinforces the material better. Two word search puzzles have words only for students who find the clue puzzles too difficult.

CROSSWORD PUZZLES
Both unit and vocabulary word sections have 4 crossword puzzles.

BINGO CARDS
There are 32 individual bingo cards for the unit words and 32 individual bingo cards for the vocabulary words. You can use your word list as a "call list," calling the words at random and marking them off of your list as you go, or you could use the flash cards by cutting them apart and drawing the words at random from a hat (or box or whatever). To make a better review, you might ask for the definition and spelling of each word as you call it out–or you could call out the definitions and have students tell you the words they need to look for on the puzzle.

JUGGLE LETTERS
The vocabulary juggle letter game is intended to help students learn the spellings of the words. One sheet has the definitions listed on it as an extra help for students who need it or to reinforce the definitions if you choose to do so.

FLASH CARDS
We've included a set of vocabulary flash cards you can duplicate, cut, and fold for your students. Some teachers make a few sets for general use by the class; others make a set for each student. Some teachers duplicate them for each student and have the students cut & fold their own. You can cut out just the words and put them in a hat, have each student pick out one word and write the definition and a sentence for that word. Students then swap words and papers, with the next student adding a sentence of his own under the last one. You can have students swap as many times as you like. Each time the student will read the sentences written prior to his own and then add a sentence. You can cut out the words and definitions separately and play "I Have; Who Has?" Each student in the room draws a word and definition. The first student says, "I have (the name of the word). Who has the definition?" The student with the definition reads it then says, "I have (the name of the vocabulary word she has). Who has the definition?" The round continues until all words and definitions have been given.

Dracula Word List

No.	Word	Clue/Definition
1.	ATTILA	Count Dracula claims to be a descendant of ___ the Hun.
2.	BACK	Renfield's is broken.
3.	BAT	Mina saw one flitting in the moonlight.
4.	BITE	These marks were found on the childrens' throats.
5.	BLOOD	Renfield laps the Doctor's off of the floor like a dog.
6.	BOXES	The Slovaks deliver large, wooden ___ with rope handles to the castle.
7.	BRIDES	The Three voluptuous women are the ___ of Dracula.
8.	BURIAL	Mina asks Jonathan to read the ___ Service for the Dead to her.
9.	CAPTAIN	The body of the ___ was tied to the wheel of the ship.
10.	CARFAX	Dracula owns ___, which is next door to Dr. Seward's place.
11.	CHILD	Jonathan hears the wail of a half-smothered ___ come from the bag.
12.	CRUCIFIX	Hotel landlady gives Jonathan this for protection
13.	DOG	A large one jumps off the ship and disappears in the dark.
14.	DRINK	Renfield stops himself before uttering this word.
15.	DUST	The purified vampires turn to this.
16.	ENGLISH	The Count wants Jonathan to teach him this.
17.	EVIL	At midnight on St. George's Day all ___ things in the world have full sway.
18.	FLOWERS	Mrs. Westerna throws away Lucy's garlic ___.
19.	GODALMING	Arthur Holmwood: Lord ___
20.	HARKER	He travels to Castle Dracula to meet with the Count about real estate.
21.	HEAD	Van Helsing wants to cut off Lucy's ___ and take out her heart.
22.	HELSING	He suggests that Lucy needs blood transfusions: Van ___
23.	HOLMWOOD	Lucy accepts his marriage proposal.
24.	HOST	Communion wafer used as a weapon against vampires
25.	LIVES	Renfield collects them.
26.	LUCY	She received 3 marriage proposals in one day.
27.	MASTER	Renfield's name for the Count
28.	MINA	She is engaged to marry Jonathan.
29.	MIND	The Count's is linked to Mina's.
30.	MIRRORS	There are none of these in the castle.
31.	NOSFERATU	The Un-Dead
32.	NOTEBOOK	Mina promises not to tell Jonathan about the contents of his ___ unless it becomes necessary.
33.	PIN	Mina thinks she accidentally pricked Lucy with one.
34.	QUINCY	American friend of Arthur Holmwood
35.	RATS	Dracula promises Renfield the lives of ___.
36.	REFLECTION	The Count has no ___ in Jonathan's mirror.
37.	SEWARD	Van Helsing instructs him to sit with Lucy through the night without leaving her.
38.	SOULS	Renfield wants life from other beings, not ___.
39.	STAKE	One is driven through Lucy's heart.
40.	STRENGTH	Jonathan marvels at the caleche driver's
41.	SUNRISE	Renfield is quiet from moonrise to ___.
42.	THREE	Number of letters the Count instructs Jonathan to write home
43.	TIGER	Van Helsing compares Dracula to one.
44.	TOMBSTONES	The old man claims these in the graveyard lie.
45.	TRANSYLVANIA	Count Dracula's home
46.	VAMPIRE	Dracula or Lucy, for example
47.	VARNA	Home port of the Demeter
48.	WESTERNA	Lucy's mother: Mrs. ___

Dracula Word List Continued

No.	Word	Clue/Definition
49.	WINDOW	The Count escapes capture at Piccadilly by jumping our of this.
50.	WOLVES	Children of the Night.

Dracula Fill in the Blanks 1

_____ 1. Mina thinks she accidentally pricked Lucy with one.

_____ 2. Mina asks Jonathan to read the ___ Service for the Dead to her.

_____ 3. Renfield is quiet from moonrise to ___.

_____ 4. Lucy accepts his marriage proposal.

_____ 5. Communion wafer used as a weapon against vampires

_____ 6. Renfield collects them.

_____ 7. American friend of Arthur Holmwood

_____ 8. Hotel landlady gives Jonathan this for protection

_____ 9. Home port of the Demeter

_____ 10. The Slovaks deliver large, wooden ___ with rope handles to the castle.

_____ 11. The old man claims these in the graveyard lie.

_____ 12. Renfield's is broken.

_____ 13. The Un-Dead

_____ 14. At midnight on St. George's Day all ___ things in the world have full sway.

_____ 15. These marks were found on the childrens' throats.

_____ 16. He suggests that Lucy needs blood transfusions: Van ___

_____ 17. Van Helsing wants to cut off Lucy's ___ and take out her heart.

_____ 18. Dracula or Lucy, for example

_____ 19. Lucy's mother: Mrs. ____

_____ 20. One is driven through Lucy's heart.

Dracula Fill in the Blanks 1 Answer Key

PIN	1. Mina thinks she accidentally pricked Lucy with one.
BURIAL	2. Mina asks Jonathan to read the ___ Service for the Dead to her.
SUNRISE	3. Renfield is quiet from moonrise to ___.
HOLMWOOD	4. Lucy accepts his marriage proposal.
HOST	5. Communion wafer used as a weapon against vampires
LIVES	6. Renfield collects them.
QUINCY	7. American friend of Arthur Holmwood
CRUCIFIX	8. Hotel landlady gives Jonathan this for protection
VARNA	9. Home port of the Demeter
BOXES	10. The Slovaks deliver large, wooden ___ with rope handles to the castle.
TOMBSTONES	11. The old man claims these in the graveyard lie.
BACK	12. Renfield's is broken.
NOSFERATU	13. The Un-Dead
EVIL	14. At midnight on St. George's Day all ___ things in the world have full sway.
BITE	15. These marks were found on the childrens' throats.
HELSING	16. He suggests that Lucy needs blood transfusions: Van ___
HEAD	17. Van Helsing wants to cut off Lucy's ___ and take out her heart.
VAMPIRE	18. Dracula or Lucy, for example
WESTERNA	19. Lucy's mother: Mrs. ____
STAKE	20. One is driven through Lucy's heart.

Dracula Fill in the Blanks 2

_____ 1. Lucy's mother: Mrs. ____

_____ 2. The body of the ___ was tied to the wheel of the ship.

_____ 3. Renfield laps the Doctor's ___ off of the floor like a dog.

_____ 4. Jonathan hears the wail of a half-smothered ___ come from the bag.

_____ 5. Children of the Night

_____ 6. He travels to Castle Dracula to meet with the Count about real estate.

_____ 7. American friend of Arthur Holmwood

_____ 8. Number of letters the Count instructs Jonathan to write home

_____ 9. Renfield wants life from other beings, not ___.

_____ 10. Hotel landlady gives Jonathan this for protection

_____ 11. Mina promises not to tell Jonathan about the contents of his ___ unless it becomes necessary.

_____ 12. One is driven through Lucy's heart.

_____ 13. At midnight on St. George's Day all ___ things in the world have full sway.

_____ 14. Renfield collects them.

_____ 15. The Count has no ___ in Jonathan's mirror.

_____ 16. Dracula promises Renfield the lives of ____.

_____ 17. Dracula owns ___, which is next door to Dr. Seward's place.

_____ 18. Van Helsing compares Dracula to one.

_____ 19. She received 3 marriage proposals in one day.

_____ 20. The Count's ___ is linked to Mina's.

Dracula Fill in the Blanks 2 Answer Key

WESTERNA	1. Lucy's mother: Mrs. ____
CAPTAIN	2. The body of the ___ was tied to the wheel of the ship.
BLOOD	3. Renfield laps the Doctor's ___ off of the floor like a dog.
CHILD	4. Jonathan hears the wail of a half-smothered ___ come from the bag.
WOLVES	5. Children of the Night
HARKER	6. He travels to Castle Dracula to meet with the Count about real estate.
QUINCY	7. American friend of Arthur Holmwood
THREE	8. Number of letters the Count instructs Jonathan to write home
SOULS	9. Renfield wants life from other beings, not ___.
CRUCIFIX	10. Hotel landlady gives Jonathan this for protection
NOTEBOOK	11. Mina promises not to tell Jonathan about the contents of his ___ unless it becomes necessary.
STAKE	12. One is driven through Lucy's heart.
EVIL	13. At midnight on St. George's Day all ___ things in the world have full sway.
LIVES	14. Renfield collects them.
REFLECTION	15. The Count has no ___ in Jonathan's mirror.
RATS	16. Dracula promises Renfield the lives of ____.
CARFAX	17. Dracula owns ___, which is next door to Dr. Seward's place.
TIGER	18. Van Helsing compares Dracula to one.
LUCY	19. She received 3 marriage proposals in one day.
MIND	20. The Count's ___ is linked to Mina's.

Dracula Fill in the Blanks 3

_____ 1. Number of letters the Count instructs Jonathan to write home

_____ 2. American friend of Arthur Holmwood

_____ 3. Home port of the Demeter

_____ 4. A large one jumps off the ship and disappears in the dark.

_____ 5. Renfield laps the Doctor's off of the floor like a dog.

_____ 6. Renfield's name for the Count

_____ 7. Van Helsing wants to cut off Lucy's ___ and take out her heart.

_____ 8. Count Dracula claims to be a descendant of ___ the Hun.

_____ 9. Mina thinks she accidentally pricked Lucy with one.

_____ 10. He suggests that Lucy needs blood transfusions: Van ___

_____ 11. She received 3 marriage proposals in one day.

_____ 12. Count Dracula's home

_____ 13. Mina promises not to tell Jonathan about the contents of his ___ unless it becomes necessary.

_____ 14. There are none of these in the castle.

_____ 15. Hotel landlady gives Jonathan this for protection

_____ 16. Lucy's mother: Mrs. ____

_____ 17. The Three voluptuous women are the ___ of Dracula.

_____ 18. Dracula or Lucy, for example

_____ 19. She is engaged to marry Jonathan.

_____ 20. Communion wafer used as a weapon against vampires

Dracula Fill in the Blanks 3 Answer Key

THREE	1. Number of letters the Count instructs Jonathan to write home
QUINCY	2. American friend of Arthur Holmwood
VARNA	3. Home port of the Demeter
DOG	4. A large one jumps off the ship and disappears in the dark.
BLOOD	5. Renfield laps the Doctor's off of the floor like a dog.
MASTER	6. Renfield's name for the Count
HEAD	7. Van Helsing wants to cut off Lucy's ___ and take out her heart.
ATTILA	8. Count Dracula claims to be a descendant of ___ the Hun.
PIN	9. Mina thinks she accidentally pricked Lucy with one.
HELSING	10. He suggests that Lucy needs blood transfusions: Van ___
LUCY	11. She received 3 marriage proposals in one day.
TRANSYLVANIA	12. Count Dracula's home
NOTEBOOK	13. Mina promises not to tell Jonathan about the contents of his ___ unless it becomes necessary.
MIRRORS	14. There are none of these in the castle.
CRUCIFIX	15. Hotel landlady gives Jonathan this for protection
WESTERNA	16. Lucy's mother: Mrs. ___
BRIDES	17. The Three voluptuous women are the ___ of Dracula.
VAMPIRE	18. Dracula or Lucy, for example
MINA	19. She is engaged to marry Jonathan.
HOST	20. Communion wafer used as a weapon against vampires

Dracula Fill in the Blanks 4

1. Count Dracula's home
2. One is driven through Lucy's heart.
3. Lucy accepts his marriage proposal.
4. Renfield is quiet from moonrise to ___.
5. The Count's is linked to Mina's.
6. Mina promises not to tell Jonathan about the contents of his ___ unless it becomes necessary.
7. The body of the ___ was tied to the wheel of the ship.
8. The old man claims these in the graveyard lie.
9. The Count escapes capture at Piccadilly by jumping our of this.
10. These marks were found on the childrens' throats.
11. The Count has no ___ in Jonathan's mirror.
12. Renfield stops himself before uttering this word.
13. A large one jumps off the ship and disappears in the dark.
14. Renfield laps the Doctor's off of the floor like a dog.
15. Van Helsing compares Dracula to one.
16. The Count wants Jonathan to teach him this.
17. Arthur Holmwood: Lord ____
18. She received 3 marriage proposals in one day.
19. Jonathan hears the wail of a half-smothered ___ come from the bag.
20. He suggests that Lucy needs blood transfusions: Van ___

Dracula Fill in the Blanks 4 Answer Key

TRANSYLVANIA	1. Count Dracula's home
STAKE	2. One is driven through Lucy's heart.
HOLMWOOD	3. Lucy accepts his marriage proposal.
SUNRISE	4. Renfield is quiet from moonrise to ___.
MIND	5. The Count's is linked to Mina's.
NOTEBOOK	6. Mina promises not to tell Jonathan about the contents of his ___ unless it becomes necessary.
CAPTAIN	7. The body of the ___ was tied to the wheel of the ship.
TOMBSTONES	8. The old man claims these in the graveyard lie.
WINDOW	9. The Count escapes capture at Piccadilly by jumping our of this.
BITE	10. These marks were found on the childrens' throats.
REFLECTION	11. The Count has no ___ in Jonathan's mirror.
DRINK	12. Renfield stops himself before uttering this word.
DOG	13. A large one jumps off the ship and disappears in the dark.
BLOOD	14. Renfield laps the Doctor's off of the floor like a dog.
TIGER	15. Van Helsing compares Dracula to one.
ENGLISH	16. The Count wants Jonathan to teach him this.
GODALMING	17. Arthur Holmwood: Lord ___
LUCY	18. She received 3 marriage proposals in one day.
CHILD	19. Jonathan hears the wail of a half-smothered ___ come from the bag.
HELSING	20. He suggests that Lucy needs blood transfusions: Van ___

Dracula Matching 1

___ 1. HOLMWOOD   A. These marks were found on the childrens' throats.
___ 2. WOLVES   B. At midnight on St. George's Day all ___ things in the world have full sway.
___ 3. TIGER   C. The body of the ___ was tied to the wheel of the ship.
___ 4. MIRRORS   D. Hotel landlady gives Jonathan this for protection
___ 5. CARFAX   E. Dracula owns ___, which is next door to Dr. Seward's place.
___ 6. BURIAL   F. Van Helsing compares Dracula to one.
___ 7. SEWARD   G. There are none of these in the castle.
___ 8. HOST   H. Renfield's is broken.
___ 9. CAPTAIN   I. Lucy accepts his marriage proposal.
___ 10. FLOWERS   J. Count Dracula claims to be a descendant of ___ the Hun.
___ 11. WINDOW   K. He travels to Castle Dracula to meet with the Count about real estate.
___ 12. ATTILA   L. The Count wants Jonathan to teach him this.
___ 13. BRIDES   M. Mina asks Jonathan to read the ___ Service for the Dead to her.
___ 14. CRUCIFIX   N. She is engaged to marry Jonathan.
___ 15. MASTER   O. The Three voluptuous women are the ___ of Dracula.
___ 16. VARNA   P. Communion wafer used as a weapon against vampires
___ 17. ENGLISH   Q. The Count escapes capture at Piccadilly by jumping our of this.
___ 18. BACK   R. Mrs. Westerna throws away Lucy's garlic ___.
___ 19. HARKER   S. Home port of the Demeter
___ 20. EVIL   T. Renfield wants life from other beings, not ___.
___ 21. STAKE   U. Van Helsing instructs him to sit with Lucy through the night without leaving her.
___ 22. MIND   V. Renfield's name for the Count
___ 23. SOULS   W. Children of the Night
___ 24. BITE   X. The Count's is linked to Mina's.
___ 25. MINA   Y. One is driven through Lucy's heart.

Dracula Matching 1 Answer Key

I -	1. HOLMWOOD	A.	These marks were found on the childrens' throats.
W -	2. WOLVES	B.	At midnight on St. George's Day all ___ things in the world have full sway.
F -	3. TIGER	C.	The body of the ___ was tied to the wheel of the ship.
G -	4. MIRRORS	D.	Hotel landlady gives Jonathan this for protection
E -	5. CARFAX	E.	Dracula owns ___, which is next door to Dr. Seward's place.
M -	6. BURIAL	F.	Van Helsing compares Dracula to one.
U -	7. SEWARD	G.	There are none of these in the castle.
P -	8. HOST	H.	Renfield's is broken.
C -	9. CAPTAIN	I.	Lucy accepts his marriage proposal.
R -	10. FLOWERS	J.	Count Dracula claims to be a descendant of ___ the Hun.
Q -	11. WINDOW	K.	He travels to Castle Dracula to meet with the Count about real estate.
J -	12. ATTILA	L.	The Count wants Jonathan to teach him this.
O -	13. BRIDES	M.	Mina asks Jonathan to read the ___ Service for the Dead to her.
D -	14. CRUCIFIX	N.	She is engaged to marry Jonathan.
V -	15. MASTER	O.	The Three voluptuous women are the ___ of Dracula.
S -	16. VARNA	P.	Communion wafer used as a weapon against vampires
L -	17. ENGLISH	Q.	The Count escapes capture at Piccadilly by jumping out of this.
H -	18. BACK	R.	Mrs. Westerna throws away Lucy's garlic ___.
K -	19. HARKER	S.	Home port of the Demeter
B -	20. EVIL	T.	Renfield wants life from other beings, not ___.
Y -	21. STAKE	U.	Van Helsing instructs him to sit with Lucy through the night without leaving her.
X -	22. MIND	V.	Renfield's name for the Count
T -	23. SOULS	W.	Children of the Night
A -	24. BITE	X.	The Count's is linked to Mina's.
N -	25. MINA	Y.	One is driven through Lucy's heart.

Dracula Matching 2

___ 1. EVIL   A. A large one jumps off the ship and disappears in the dark.
___ 2. BAT   B. Dracula or Lucy, for example
___ 3. SOULS   C. The Slovaks deliver large, wooden ___ with rope handles to the castle.
___ 4. BACK   D. Renfield's name for the Count
___ 5. WINDOW   E. Jonathan marvels at the caleche driver's
___ 6. HARKER   F. Renfield's is broken.
___ 7. CHILD   G. Renfield wants life from other beings, not ___.
___ 8. TIGER   H. Arthur Holmwood: Lord ____
___ 9. STRENGTH   I. Mina saw one flitting in the moonlight.
___ 10. HEAD   J. Number of letters the Count instructs Jonathan to write home
___ 11. DOG   K. These marks were found on the childrens' throats.
___ 12. WOLVES   L. Van Helsing compares Dracula to one.
___ 13. LIVES   M. The Count's is linked to Mina's.
___ 14. LUCY   N. Van Helsing instructs him to sit with Lucy through the night without leaving her.
___ 15. VAMPIRE   O. He travels to Castle Dracula to meet with the Count about real estate.
___ 16. PIN   P. Jonathan hears the wail of a half-smothered ___ come from the bag.
___ 17. BOXES   Q. Renfield collects them.
___ 18. SEWARD   R. She is engaged to marry Jonathan.
___ 19. HOST   S. Van Helsing wants to cut off Lucy's ___ and take out her heart.
___ 20. BITE   T. At midnight on St. George's Day all ___ things in the world have full sway.
___ 21. MASTER   U. Communion wafer used as a weapon against vampires
___ 22. MINA   V. She received 3 marriage proposals in one day.
___ 23. THREE   W. Children of the Night
___ 24. GODALMING   X. The Count escapes capture at Piccadilly by jumping our of this.
___ 25. MIND   Y. Mina thinks she accidentally pricked Lucy with one.

Dracula Matching 2 Answer Key

T - 1. EVIL	A. A large one jumps off the ship and disappears in the dark.
I - 2. BAT	B. Dracula or Lucy, for example
G - 3. SOULS	C. The Slovaks deliver large, wooden ___ with rope handles to the castle.
F - 4. BACK	D. Renfield's name for the Count
X - 5. WINDOW	E. Jonathan marvels at the caleche driver's
O - 6. HARKER	F. Renfield's is broken.
P - 7. CHILD	G. Renfield wants life from other beings, not ___.
L - 8. TIGER	H. Arthur Holmwood: Lord ___
E - 9. STRENGTH	I. Mina saw one flitting in the moonlight.
S - 10. HEAD	J. Number of letters the Count instructs Jonathan to write home
A - 11. DOG	K. These marks were found on the childrens' throats.
W - 12. WOLVES	L. Van Helsing compares Dracula to one.
Q - 13. LIVES	M. The Count's is linked to Mina's.
V - 14. LUCY	N. Van Helsing instructs him to sit with Lucy through the night without leaving her.
B - 15. VAMPIRE	O. He travels to Castle Dracula to meet with the Count about real estate.
Y - 16. PIN	P. Jonathan hears the wail of a half-smothered ___ come from the bag.
C - 17. BOXES	Q. Renfield collects them.
N - 18. SEWARD	R. She is engaged to marry Jonathan.
U - 19. HOST	S. Van Helsing wants to cut off Lucy's ___ and take out her heart.
K - 20. BITE	T. At midnight on St. George's Day all ___ things in the world have full sway.
D - 21. MASTER	U. Communion wafer used as a weapon against vampires
R - 22. MINA	V. She received 3 marriage proposals in one day.
J - 23. THREE	W. Children of the Night
H - 24. GODALMING	X. The Count escapes capture at Piccadilly by jumping our of this.
M - 25. MIND	Y. Mina thinks she accidentally pricked Lucy with one.

Dracula Matching 3

___ 1. GODALMING
___ 2. DRINK
___ 3. REFLECTION
___ 4. ATTILA
___ 5. CARFAX
___ 6. THREE
___ 7. FLOWERS
___ 8. HEAD
___ 9. ENGLISH
___ 10. HOST
___ 11. RATS
___ 12. NOTEBOOK
___ 13. SEWARD
___ 14. TRANSYLVANIA
___ 15. SUNRISE
___ 16. DOG
___ 17. BLOOD
___ 18. WINDOW
___ 19. EVIL
___ 20. SOULS
___ 21. HELSING
___ 22. BURIAL
___ 23. HOLMWOOD
___ 24. STRENGTH
___ 25. CHILD

A. He suggests that Lucy needs blood transfusions: Van ___
B. Van Helsing instructs him to sit with Lucy through the night without leaving her.
C. Arthur Holmwood: Lord ____
D. Renfield wants life from other beings, not ___.
E. Renfield stops himself before uttering this word.
F. Dracula owns ___, which is next door to Dr. Seward's place.
G. The Count wants Jonathan to teach him this.
H. Count Dracula's home
I. Renfield is quiet from moonrise to ___.
J. The Count escapes capture at Piccadilly by jumping our of this.
K. Jonathan hears the wail of a half-smothered ___ come from the bag.
L. Van Helsing wants to cut off Lucy's ___ and take out her heart.
M. At midnight on St. George's Day all ___ things in the world have full sway.
N. Dracula promises Renfield the lives of ____.
O. Jonathan marvels at the caleche driver's
P. Lucy accepts his marriage proposal.
Q. Communion wafer used as a weapon against vampires
R. Mrs. Westerna throws away Lucy's garlic ___.
S. The Count has no ___ in Jonathan's mirror.
T. Count Dracula claims to be a descendant of ___ the Hun.
U. Mina asks Jonathan to read the ___ Service for the Dead to her.
V. A large one jumps off the ship and disappears in the dark.
W. Renfield laps the Doctor's off of the floor like a dog.
X. Number of letters the Count instructs Jonathan to write home
Y. Mina promises not to tell Jonathan about the contents of his ___ unless it becomes necessary.

Dracula Matching 3 Answer Key

C - 1. GODALMING	A.	He suggests that Lucy needs blood transfusions: Van ___
E - 2. DRINK	B.	Van Helsing instructs him to sit with Lucy through the night without leaving her.
S - 3. REFLECTION	C.	Arthur Holmwood: Lord ___
T - 4. ATTILA	D.	Renfield wants life from other beings, not ___.
F - 5. CARFAX	E.	Renfield stops himself before uttering this word.
X - 6. THREE	F.	Dracula owns ___, which is next door to Dr. Seward's place.
R - 7. FLOWERS	G.	The Count wants Jonathan to teach him this.
L - 8. HEAD	H.	Count Dracula's home
G - 9. ENGLISH	I.	Renfield is quiet from moonrise to ___.
Q -10. HOST	J.	The Count escapes capture at Piccadilly by jumping out of this.
N -11. RATS	K.	Jonathan hears the wail of a half-smothered ___ come from the bag.
Y -12. NOTEBOOK	L.	Van Helsing wants to cut off Lucy's ___ and take out her heart.
B -13. SEWARD	M.	At midnight on St. George's Day all ___ things in the world have full sway.
H -14. TRANSYLVANIA	N.	Dracula promises Renfield the lives of ___.
I -15. SUNRISE	O.	Jonathan marvels at the caleche driver's
V -16. DOG	P.	Lucy accepts his marriage proposal.
W -17. BLOOD	Q.	Communion wafer used as a weapon against vampires
J -18. WINDOW	R.	Mrs. Westerna throws away Lucy's garlic ___.
M -19. EVIL	S.	The Count has no ___ in Jonathan's mirror.
D -20. SOULS	T.	Count Dracula claims to be a descendant of ___ the Hun.
A -21. HELSING	U.	Mina asks Jonathan to read the ___ Service for the Dead to her.
U -22. BURIAL	V.	A large one jumps off the ship and disappears in the dark.
P -23. HOLMWOOD	W.	Renfield laps the Doctor's off of the floor like a dog.
O -24. STRENGTH	X.	Number of letters the Count instructs Jonathan to write home
K -25. CHILD	Y.	Mina promises not to tell Jonathan about the contents of his ___ unless it becomes necessary.

Dracula Matching 4

___ 1. VARNA   A. Renfield's is broken.
___ 2. MIRRORS   B. Home port of the Demeter
___ 3. STRENGTH   C. He travels to Castle Dracula to meet with the Count about real estate.
___ 4. MASTER   D. Count Dracula's home
___ 5. WINDOW   E. The Count's is linked to Mina's.
___ 6. SUNRISE   F. The Un-Dead
___ 7. WOLVES   G. Lucy's mother: Mrs. ____
___ 8. HEAD   H. Van Helsing wants to cut off Lucy's ___ and take out her heart.
___ 9. HELSING   I. There are none of these in the castle.
___ 10. NOSFERATU   J. Renfield's name for the Count
___ 11. BLOOD   K. Mrs. Westerna throws away Lucy's garlic ___.
___ 12. FLOWERS   L. The purified vampires turn to this.
___ 13. MIND   M. She received 3 marriage proposals in one day.
___ 14. LUCY   N. Mina thinks she accidentally pricked Lucy with one.
___ 15. RATS   O. The Count escapes capture at Piccadilly by jumping our of this.
___ 16. BACK   P. She is engaged to marry Jonathan.
___ 17. TRANSYLVANIA   Q. He suggests that Lucy needs blood transfusions: Van ___
___ 18. HARKER   R. Dracula promises Renfield the lives of ____.
___ 19. PIN   S. The Three voluptuous women are the ___ of Dracula.
___ 20. WESTERNA   T. Children of the Night
___ 21. BRIDES   U. A large one jumps off the ship and disappears in the dark.
___ 22. STAKE   V. Renfield laps the Doctor's off of the floor like a dog.
___ 23. DUST   W. Jonathan marvels at the caleche driver's
___ 24. DOG   X. One is driven through Lucy's heart.
___ 25. MINA   Y. Renfield is quiet from moonrise to ___.

Dracula Matching 4 Answer Key

B - 1. VARNA	A.	Renfield's is broken.
I - 2. MIRRORS	B.	Home port of the Demeter
W - 3. STRENGTH	C.	He travels to Castle Dracula to meet with the Count about real estate.
J - 4. MASTER	D.	Count Dracula's home
O - 5. WINDOW	E.	The Count's is linked to Mina's.
Y - 6. SUNRISE	F.	The Un-Dead
T - 7. WOLVES	G.	Lucy's mother: Mrs. ____
H - 8. HEAD	H.	Van Helsing wants to cut off Lucy's ___ and take out her heart.
Q - 9. HELSING	I.	There are none of these in the castle.
F - 10. NOSFERATU	J.	Renfield's name for the Count
V - 11. BLOOD	K.	Mrs. Westerna throws away Lucy's garlic ___.
K - 12. FLOWERS	L.	The purified vampires turn to this.
E - 13. MIND	M.	She received 3 marriage proposals in one day.
M - 14. LUCY	N.	Mina thinks she accidentally pricked Lucy with one.
R - 15. RATS	O.	The Count escapes capture at Piccadilly by jumping our of this.
A - 16. BACK	P.	She is engaged to marry Jonathan.
D - 17. TRANSYLVANIA	Q.	He suggests that Lucy needs blood transfusions: Van ___
C - 18. HARKER	R.	Dracula promises Renfield the lives of ____.
N - 19. PIN	S.	The Three voluptuous women are the ___ of Dracula.
G - 20. WESTERNA	T.	Children of the Night
S - 21. BRIDES	U.	A large one jumps off the ship and disappears in the dark.
X - 22. STAKE	V.	Renfield laps the Doctor's off of the floor like a dog.
L - 23. DUST	W.	Jonathan marvels at the caleche driver's
U - 24. DOG	X.	One is driven through Lucy's heart.
P - 25. MINA	Y.	Renfield is quiet from moonrise to ___.

Dracula Magic Squares 1

Match the definition with the vocabulary word. Put your answers in the magic squares below. When your answers are correct, all columns and rows will add to the same number.

A. SOULS
B. TIGER
C. MIND
D. STRENGTH
E. BAT
F. SUNRISE
G. PIN
H. LUCY
I. CHILD
J. GODALMING
K. WOLVES
L. ATTILA
M. HELSING
N. VAMPIRE
O. CRUCIFIX
P. SEWARD

1. The Count's is linked to Mina's.
2. Arthur Holmwood: Lord ____
3. Renfield is quiet from moonrise to ___.
4. Hotel landlady gives Jonathan this for protection
5. Van Helsing instructs him to sit with Lucy through the night without leaving her.
6. Mina saw one flitting in the moonlight.
7. Jonathan hears the wail of a half-smothered ___ come from the bag.
8. Jonathan marvels at the caleche driver's
9. He suggests that Lucy needs blood transfusions: Van ___
10. She received 3 marriage proposals in one day.
11. Count Dracula claims to be a descendant of ___ the Hun.
12. Renfield wants life from other beings, not ___.
13. Van Helsing compares Dracula to one.
14. Children of the Night
15. Mina thinks she accidentally pricked Lucy with one.
16. Dracula or Lucy, for example

A=	B=	C=	D=
E=	F=	G=	H=
I=	J=	K=	L=
M=	N=	O=	P=

Dracula Magic Squares 1 Answer Key

Match the definition with the vocabulary word. Put your answers in the magic squares below. When your answers are correct, all columns and rows will add to the same number.

A. SOULS
B. TIGER
C. MIND
D. STRENGTH
E. BAT
F. SUNRISE
G. PIN
H. LUCY
I. CHILD
J. GODALMING
K. WOLVES
L. ATTILA
M. HELSING
N. VAMPIRE
O. CRUCIFIX
P. SEWARD

1. The Count's is linked to Mina's.
2. Arthur Holmwood: Lord ____
3. Renfield is quiet from moonrise to ____.
4. Hotel landlady gives Jonathan this for protection
5. Van Helsing instructs him to sit with Lucy through the night without leaving her.
6. Mina saw one flitting in the moonlight.
7. Jonathan hears the wail of a half-smothered ____ come from the bag.
8. Jonathan marvels at the caleche driver's
9. He suggests that Lucy needs blood transfusions: Van ____
10. She received 3 marriage proposals in one day.
11. Count Dracula claims to be a descendant of ____ the Hun.
12. Renfield wants life from other beings, not ____.
13. Van Helsing compares Dracula to one.
14. Children of the Night
15. Mina thinks she accidentally pricked Lucy with one.
16. Dracula or Lucy, for example

A=12	B=13	C=1	D=8
E=6	F=3	G=15	H=10
I=7	J=2	K=14	L=11
M=9	N=16	O=4	P=5

Dracula Magic Squares 2

Match the definition with the vocabulary word. Put your answers in the magic squares below. When your answers are correct, all columns and rows will add to the same number.

A. NOTEBOOK   E. BACK   I. WINDOW   M. REFLECTION
B. BAT   F. RATS   J. DRINK   N. TOMBSTONES
C. SEWARD   G. HOST   K. QUINCY   O. THREE
D. SUNRISE   H. MASTER   L. STRENGTH   P. HELSING

1. Mina promises not to tell Jonathan about the contents of his ___ unless it becomes necessary.
2. The old man claims these in the graveyard lie.
3. Renfield stops himself before uttering this word.
4. Renfield's is broken.
5. Communion wafer used as a weapon against vampires
6. Jonathan marvels at the caleche driver's
7. He suggests that Lucy needs blood transfusions: Van ___
8. Van Helsing instructs him to sit with Lucy through the night without leaving her.
9. Number of letters the Count instructs Jonathan to write home
10. Renfield is quiet from moonrise to ___.
11. Renfield's name for the Count
12. American friend of Arthur Holmwood
13. The Count escapes capture at Piccadilly by jumping our of this.
14. Dracula promises Renfield the lives of ____.
15. Mina saw one flitting in the moonlight.
16. The Count has no ___ in Jonathan's mirror.

A=	B=	C=	D=
E=	F=	G=	H=
I=	J=	K=	L=
M=	N=	O=	P=

Dracula Magic Squares 2 Answer Key

Match the definition with the vocabulary word. Put your answers in the magic squares below. When your answers are correct, all columns and rows will add to the same number.

A. NOTEBOOK
B. BAT
C. SEWARD
D. SUNRISE
E. BACK
F. RATS
G. HOST
H. MASTER
I. WINDOW
J. DRINK
K. QUINCY
L. STRENGTH
M. REFLECTION
N. TOMBSTONES
O. THREE
P. HELSING

1. Mina promises not to tell Jonathan about the contents of his ___ unless it becomes necessary.
2. The old man claims these in the graveyard lie.
3. Renfield stops himself before uttering this word.
4. Renfield's is broken.
5. Communion wafer used as a weapon against vampires
6. Jonathan marvels at the caleche driver's
7. He suggests that Lucy needs blood transfusions: Van ___
8. Van Helsing instructs him to sit with Lucy through the night without leaving her.
9. Number of letters the Count instructs Jonathan to write home
10. Renfield is quiet from moonrise to ___.
11. Renfield's name for the Count
12. American friend of Arthur Holmwood
13. The Count escapes capture at Piccadilly by jumping our of this.
14. Dracula promises Renfield the lives of ____.
15. Mina saw one flitting in the moonlight.
16. The Count has no ___ in Jonathan's mirror.

A=1	B=15	C=8	D=10
E=4	F=14	G=5	H=11
I=13	J=3	K=12	L=6
M=16	N=2	O=9	P=7

Dracula Magic Squares 3

Match the definition with the vocabulary word. Put your answers in the magic squares below. When your answers are correct, all columns and rows will add to the same number.

A. MASTER   E. ATTILA   I. ENGLISH   M. CAPTAIN
B. TIGER   F. NOSFERATU   J. FLOWERS   N. HEAD
C. EVIL   G. BOXES   K. SEWARD   O. BLOOD
D. WINDOW   H. CRUCIFIX   L. MIRRORS   P. DOG

1. Hotel landlady gives Jonathan this for protection
2. Renfield's name for the Count
3. Van Helsing compares Dracula to one.
4. The Slovaks deliver large, wooden ___ with rope handles to the castle.
5. Mrs. Westerna throws away Lucy's garlic ___.
6. Renfield laps the Doctor's off of the floor like a dog.
7. A large one jumps off the ship and disappears in the dark.
8. The Count wants Jonathan to teach him this.
9. Van Helsing instructs him to sit with Lucy through the night without leaving her.
10. Van Helsing wants to cut off Lucy's ___ and take out her heart.
11. The body of the ___ was tied to the wheel of the ship.
12. There are none of these in the castle.
13. Count Dracula claims to be a descendant of ___ the Hun.
14. The Count escapes capture at Piccadilly by jumping our of this.
15. At midnight on St. George's Day all ___ things in the world have full sway.
16. The Un-Dead

A=	B=	C=	D=
E=	F=	G=	H=
I=	J=	K=	L=
M=	N=	O=	P=

Dracula Magic Squares 3 Answer Key

Match the definition with the vocabulary word. Put your answers in the magic squares below. When your answers are correct, all columns and rows will add to the same number.

A. MASTER
B. TIGER
C. EVIL
D. WINDOW
E. ATTILA
F. NOSFERATU
G. BOXES
H. CRUCIFIX
I. ENGLISH
J. FLOWERS
K. SEWARD
L. MIRRORS
M. CAPTAIN
N. HEAD
O. BLOOD
P. DOG

1. Hotel landlady gives Jonathan this for protection
2. Renfield's name for the Count
3. Van Helsing compares Dracula to one.
4. The Slovaks deliver large, wooden ___ with rope handles to the castle.
5. Mrs. Westerna throws away Lucy's garlic ___.
6. Renfield laps the Doctor's off of the floor like a dog.
7. A large one jumps off the ship and disappears in the dark.
8. The Count wants Jonathan to teach him this.
9. Van Helsing instructs him to sit with Lucy through the night without leaving her.
10. Van Helsing wants to cut off Lucy's ___ and take out her heart.
11. The body of the ___ was tied to the wheel of the ship.
12. There are none of these in the castle.
13. Count Dracula claims to be a descendant of ___ the Hun.
14. The Count escapes capture at Piccadilly by jumping our of this.
15. At midnight on St. George's Day all ___ things in the world have full sway.
16. The Un-Dead

A=2	B=3	C=15	D=14
E=13	F=16	G=4	H=1
I=8	J=5	K=9	L=12
M=11	N=10	O=6	P=7

Dracula Magic Squares 4

Match the definition with the vocabulary word. Put your answers in the magic squares below. When your answers are correct, all columns and rows will add to the same number.

A. NOSFERATU   E. STAKE   I. DOG   M. REFLECTION
B. MINA   F. CHILD   J. THREE   N. PIN
C. TRANSYLVANIA   G. SOULS   K. STRENGTH   O. TOMBSTONES
D. HOLMWOOD   H. WOLVES   L. SUNRISE   P. DRINK

1. The Count has no ___ in Jonathan's mirror.
2. Jonathan hears the wail of a half-smothered ___ come from the bag.
3. Children of the Night
4. The old man claims these in the graveyard lie.
5. Renfield is quiet from moonrise to ___.
6. Count Dracula's home
7. The Un-Dead
8. Number of letters the Count instructs Jonathan to write home
9. Jonathan marvels at the caleche driver's
10. Lucy accepts his marriage proposal.
11. She is engaged to marry Jonathan.
12. A large one jumps off the ship and disappears in the dark.
13. Mina thinks she accidentally pricked Lucy with one.
14. One is driven through Lucy's heart.
15. Renfield wants life from other beings, not ___.
16. Renfield stops himself before uttering this word.

A=	B=	C=	D=
E=	F=	G=	H=
I=	J=	K=	L=
M=	N=	O=	P=

Dracula Magic Squares 4 Answer Key

Match the definition with the vocabulary word. Put your answers in the magic squares below. When your answers are correct, all columns and rows will add to the same number.

A. NOSFERATU   E. STAKE   I. DOG   M. REFLECTION
B. MINA   F. CHILD   J. THREE N. PIN
C. TRANSYLVANIA G. SOULS   K. STRENGTH O. TOMBSTONES
D. HOLMWOOD   H. WOLVES   L. SUNRISE P. DRINK

1. The Count has no ___ in Jonathan's mirror.
2. Jonathan hears the wail of a half-smothered ___ come from the bag
3. Children of the Night
4. The old man claims these in the graveyard lie.
5. Renfield is quiet from moonrise to ___.
6. Count Dracula's home
7. The Un-Dead
8. Number of letters the Count instructs Jonathan to write home
9. Jonathan marvels at the caleche driver's
10. Lucy accepts his marriage proposal.
11. She is engaged to marry Jonathan.
12. A large one jumps off the ship and disappears in the dark.
13. Mina thinks she accidentally pricked Lucy with one.
14. One is driven through Lucy's heart.
15. Renfield wants life from other beings, not ___.
16. Renfield stops himself before uttering this word.

A=7	B=11	C=6	D=10
E=14	F=2	G=15	H=3
I=12	J=8	K=9	L=5
M=1	N=13	O=4	P=16

Dracula Word Search 1

```
M I R R O R S L A I R U B S E V I L
M D M F W H V N G E M X K E T G G Z
B R I D E S R J K J A M R N I Z H V
D Q N G W E D R F A S H E D B Y K G
K H A R T O A D L U T A R E F S O N
C R O S O H L I O V E S I Q L M M Y
K C E L B L T V W S R K P F K L V H
S W B Z M T F S E D G Q M X D X D P
N Q V K A W B R R S N C A R F A X H
X D U V M N O I S N I W V B K D V G
L S R I Y K N O E M S I L C F R A G
B X E Z N K L S D I L N G A G A R F
A G G L V C I B S N E D S P S W N C
C H I L D R Y G O D H O S T H E A D
K V T G N C C T U X L W A A A S D L
E J M U U R A S L J E R R I N K D T
N G S L X B T Y S R Q S R N I P E G
```

A large one jumps off the ship and disappears in the dark. (3)
American friend of Arthur Holmwood (6)
At midnight on St. George's Day all ___ things in the world have full sway. (4)
Children of the Night (6)
Communion wafer used as a weapon against vampires (4)
Count Dracula claims to be a descendant of ___ the Hun. (6)
Dracula or Lucy, for example (7)
Dracula owns ___, which is next door to Dr. Seward's place. (6)
Dracula promises Renfield the lives of ____. (4)
He suggests that Lucy needs blood transfusions: Van ___ (7)
He travels to Castle Dracula to meet with the Count about real estate. (6)
Home port of the Demeter (5)
Jonathan hears the wail of a half-smothered ___ come from the bag. (5)
Lucy accepts his marriage proposal. (8)
Lucy's mother: Mrs. ____ (8)
Mina asks Jonathan to read the ___ Service for the Dead to her. (6)
Mina saw one flitting in the moonlight. (3)
Mina thinks she accidentally pricked Lucy with one. (3)
Mrs. Westerna throws away Lucy's garlic ___. (7)
Number of letters the Count instructs Jonathan to write home (5)

One is driven through Lucy's heart. (5)
Renfield collects them. (5)
Renfield is quiet from moonrise to ___. (7)
Renfield laps the Doctor's off of the floor like a dog. (5)
Renfield stops himself before uttering this word. (5)
Renfield wants life from other beings, not ___. (5)
Renfield's is broken. (4)
Renfield's name for the Count (6)
She is engaged to marry Jonathan. (4)
She received 3 marriage proposals in one day. (4)
The Count escapes capture at Piccadilly by jumping our of this. (6)
The Count's is linked to Mina's. (4)
The Slovaks deliver large, wooden ___ with rope handles to the castle. (5)
The Three voluptuous women are the ___ of Dracula. (6)
The Un-Dead (9)
The body of the ___ was tied to the wheel of the ship. (7)
The purified vampires turn to this. (4)
There are none of these in the castle. (7)
These marks were found on the childrens' throats. (4)
Van Helsing compares Dracula to one. (5)
Van Helsing instructs him to sit with Lucy through the night without leaving her. (6)
Van Helsing wants to cut off Lucy's ___ and take out her heart. (4)

Dracula Word Search 1 Answer Key

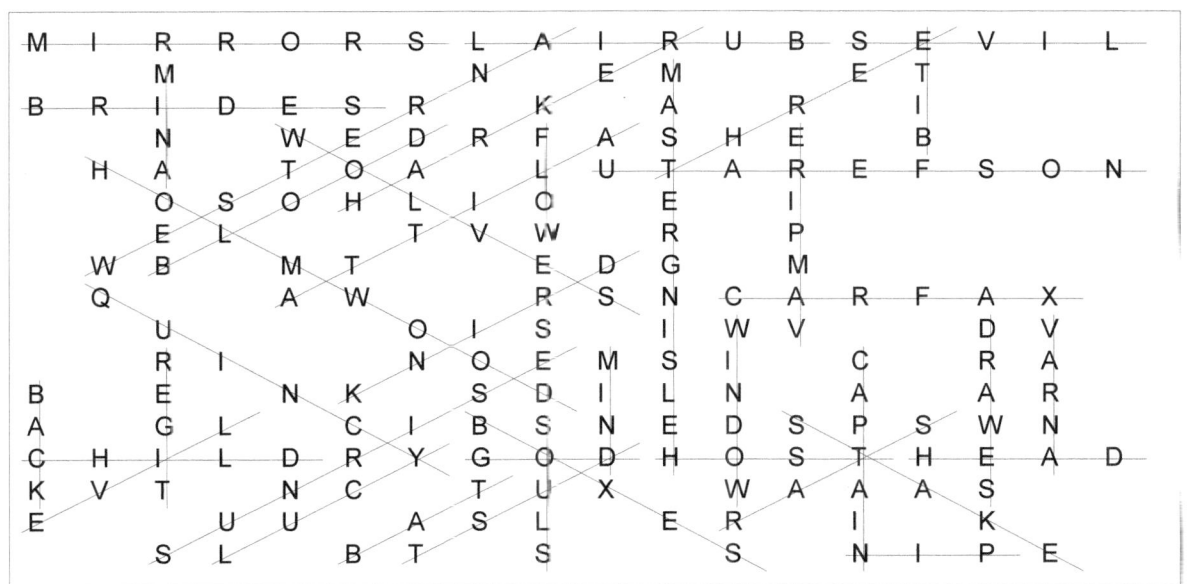

A large one jumps off the ship and disappears in the dark. (3)
American friend of Arthur Holmwood (6)
At midnight on St. George's Day all ___ things n the world have full sway. (4)
Children of the Night (6)
Communion wafer used as a weapon against vampires (4)
Count Dracula claims to be a descendant of ___ the Hun. (6)
Dracula or Lucy, for example (7)
Dracula owns ___, which is next door to Dr. Seward's place. (6)
Dracula promises Renfield the lives of ____. (4)
He suggests that Lucy needs blood transfusions: Van ___ (7)
He travels to Castle Dracula to meet with the Count about real estate. (6)
Home port of the Demeter (5)
Jonathan hears the wail of a half-smothered ___ come from the bag. (5)
Lucy accepts his marriage proposal. (8)
Lucy's mother: Mrs. ____ (8)
Mina asks Jonathan to read the ___ Service for the Dead to her. (6)
Mina saw one flitting in the moonlight. (3)
Mina thinks she accidentally pricked Lucy with one. (3)
Mrs. Westerna throws away Lucy's garlic ___. (7)
Number of letters the Count instructs Jonathan to write home (5)

One is driven through Lucy's heart. (5)
Renfield collects them. (5)
Renfield is quiet from moonrise to ___. (7)
Renfield laps the Doctor's off of the floor like a dog. (5)
Renfield stops himself before uttering this word. (5)
Renfield wants life from other beings, not ___. (5)
Renfield's is broken. (4)
Renfield's name for the Count (6)
She is engaged to marry Jonathan. (4)
She received 3 marriage proposals in one day. (4)
The Count escapes capture at Piccadilly by jumping our of this. (6)
The Count's is linked to Mina's. (4)
The Slovaks deliver large, wooden ___ with rope handles to the castle. (5)
The Three voluptuous women are the ___ of Dracula. (6)
The Un-Dead (9)
The body of the ___ was tied to the wheel of the ship. (7)
The purified vampires turn to this. (4)
There are none of these in the castle. (7)
These marks were found on the childrens' throats. (4)
Van Helsing compares Dracula to one. (5)
Van Helsing instructs him to sit with Lucy through the night without leaving her. (6)
Van Helsing wants to cut off Lucy's ___ and take out her heart. (4)

Dracula Word Search 2

```
V S T R E N G T H F L O W E R S D X
Y A Z B Q L T S E M H A R K E R Y G
T J R T I T I Q A I B W T T B O X H
D R I N K T G V D N O P G Z H R W E
R E T S A M E S E D I R B X V R S Z
V K V B B K R P N S H R A K A I E T
Y V W I A T T I L A W F F T R M R E
C N C T L S W N L G R Y S N G A N T
H O S T H E W N Z A D S U N N G N M
Q S E T O N N P C L E S I S N I W G
W F X B L O O D I V Q M Y I P D C K
J E O V M T W H L H L L S K L A R K
N R B B W S C O S A V L N A P T G J
R A J Z O B W L D A E R I T D L Y R
B T S H O M U O N H N R A N U U Y T
S U F G D O G I K Q U I N C Y J S W
B A C K S T A B Y B N H Y M I N A T
```

A large one jumps off the ship and disappears in the dark. (3)
American friend of Arthur Holmwood (6)
Arthur Holmwood: Lord ____ (9)
At midnight on St. George's Day all ___ things in the world have full sway. (4)
Children of the Night (6)
Communion wafer used as a weapon against vampires (4)
Count Dracula claims to be a descendant of ___ the Hun. (6)
Count Dracula's home (12)
Dracula owns ___, which is next door to Dr. Seward's place. (6)
Dracula promises Renfield the lives of ____. (4)
He suggests that Lucy needs blood transfusions: Van ___ (7)
He travels to Castle Dracula to meet with the Count about real estate. (6)
Home port of the Demeter (5)
Jonathan hears the wail of a half-smothered ___ come from the bag. (5)
Jonathan marvels at the caleche driver's (8)
Lucy accepts his marriage proposal. (8)
Mina asks Jonathan to read the ___ Service for the Dead to her. (6)
Mina saw one flitting in the moonlight. (3)
Mina thinks she accidentally pricked Lucy with one. (3)
Mrs. Westerna throws away Lucy's garlic ___. (7)
Number of letters the Count instructs Jonathan to write home (5)
One is driven through Lucy's heart. (5)
Renfield collects them. (5)
Renfield is quiet from moonrise to ___. (7)
Renfield laps the Doctor's off of the floor like a dog. (5)
Renfield stops himself before uttering this word. (5)
Renfield wants life from other beings, not ___. (5)
Renfield's is broken. (4)
Renfield's name for the Count (6)
She is engaged to marry Jonathan. (4)
She received 3 marriage proposals in one day. (4)
The Count escapes capture at Piccadilly by jumping our of this. (6)
The Count's is linked to Mina's. (4)
The Slovaks deliver large, wooden ___ with rope handles to the castle. (5)
The Three voluptuous women are the ___ of Dracula. (6)
The Un-Dead (9)
The body of the ___ was tied to the wheel of the ship. (7)
The old man claims these in the graveyard lie. (10)
The purified vampires turn to this. (4)
There are none of these in the castle. (7)
These marks were found on the childrens' throats. (4)
Van Helsing compares Dracula to one. (5)
Van Helsing wants to cut off Lucy's ___ and take out her heart. (4)

Dracula Word Search 2 Answer Key

A large one jumps off the ship and disappears in the dark. (3)
American friend of Arthur Holmwood (6)
Arthur Holmwood: Lord ____ (9)
At midnight on St. George's Day all ___ things in the world have full sway. (4)
Children of the Night (6)
Communion wafer used as a weapon against vampires (4)
Count Dracula claims to be a descendant of ___ the Hun. (6)
Count Dracula's home (12)
Dracula owns ___, which is next door to Dr. Seward's place. (6)
Dracula promises Renfield the lives of ____. (4)
He suggests that Lucy needs blood transfusions: Van ___ (7)
He travels to Castle Dracula to meet with the Count about real estate. (6)
Home port of the Demeter (5)
Jonathan hears the wail of a half-smothered ___ come from the bag. (5)
Jonathan marvels at the caleche driver's (8)
Lucy accepts his marriage proposal. (8)
Mina asks Jonathan to read the ___ Service for the Dead to her. (6)
Mina saw one flitting in the moonlight. (3)
Mina thinks she accidentally pricked Lucy with one. (3)
Mrs. Westerna throws away Lucy's garlic ___. (7)
Number of letters the Count instructs Jonathan to write home (5)
One is driven through Lucy's heart. (5)
Renfield collects them. (5)
Renfield is quiet from moonrise to ___. (7)
Renfield laps the Doctor's off of the floor like a dog. (5)
Renfield stops himself before uttering this word. (5)
Renfield wants life from other beings, not ___. (5)
Renfield's is broken. (4)
Renfield's name for the Count (6)
She is engaged to marry Jonathan. (4)
She received 3 marriage proposals in one day. (4)
The Count escapes capture at Piccadilly by jumping our of this. (6)
The Count's is linked to Mina's. (4)
The Slovaks deliver large, wooden ___ with rope handles to the castle. (5)
The Three voluptuous women are the ___ of Dracula. (6)
The Un-Dead (9)
The body of the ___ was tied to the wheel of the ship. (7)
The old man claims these in the graveyard lie. (10)
The purified vampires turn to this. (4)
There are none of these in the castle. (7)
These marks were found on the childrens' throats. (4)
Van Helsing compares Dracula to one. (5)
Van Helsing wants to cut off Lucy's ___ and take out her heart. (4)

Dracula Word Search 3

```
W M V D O O L B V W B W E S T E R N A J
A I W D U L H P F M Z R S W D Q K V P
T B N Z J S M M W J D O I G O Z O B A D
T X H D I K T Q R L R R F D P U Z G M P
I C X L O C G E H R A N L L E H L T P T
L W G K V W K P I M W R O U Q S P S I F
A N C G D R L M B V E L W C U K N I R D
E A X L A F I A J G S I E Y I P Q A E D
B B I H D N V S I C V V R X N S T M N B
H H U B D S E T Z G J E S N C S R M O H
C R M R A P K E C Q D S H N Y F A L T W
G Z V G I T L R Z A N G Y Y K V N F E V
Z B Y L M A R N P G P V T T N S S D B V
C L C J F Q L N W W C T Z S H L Y S O C
Q H O L M W O O D S N X A X R X L B O Y
N R P H V H Y S F Z S N M I L G V G K X
M F Y Y Q Q L F X U Y Z V F N O A L W K
T Z L J W T T E N V V G H I G D N M O H
X H L M A H Y R K P C N T C Y A I W L W
S S R N S O I A N J A I G U B L A P V R
X T R E S S Y T R Y R S N R B M M I E R
D A E H E T Y U R E F L E C T I O N S L
V K M W X H W K B L A E R L N N T H K D
D E H Q O Y C G W Y X H T A T G S E R G
Z G S X B L H V T O M B S T O N E S Z P
```

ATTILA	CHILD	HEAD	NOSFERATU	SUNRISE
BACK	CRUCIFIX	HELSING	NOTEBOOK	THREE
BAT	DOG	HOLMWOOD	PIN	TIGER
BITE	DRINK	HOST	QUINCY	TOMBSTONES
BLOOD	DUST	LIVES	RATS	TRANSYLVANIA
BOXES	ENGLISH	LUCY	REFLECTION	VAMPIRE
BRIDES	EVIL	MASTER	SEWARD	VARNA
BURIAL	FLOWERS	MINA	SOULS	WESTERNA
CAPTAIN	GODALMING	MIND	STAKE	WINDOW
CARFAX	HARKER	MIRRORS	STRENGTH	WOLVES

Dracula Word Search 3 Answer Key

ATTILA	CHILD	HEAD	NOSFERATU	SUNRISE
BACK	CRUCIFIX	HELSING	NOTEBOOK	THREE
BAT	DOG	HOLMWOOD	PIN	TIGER
BITE	DRINK	HOST	QUINCY	TOMBSTONES
BLOOD	DUST	LIVES	RATS	TRANSYLVANIA
BOXES	ENGLISH	LUCY	REFLECTION	VAMPIRE
BRIDES	EVIL	MASTER	SEWARD	VARNA
BURIAL	FLOWERS	MINA	SOULS	WESTERNA
CAPTAIN	GODALMING	MIND	STAKE	WINDOW
CARFAX	HARKER	MIRRORS	STRENGTH	WOLVES

Dracula Word Search 4

```
L I V E S H O L M W O O D V A M P I R E
G P T L R Q J I Y I O Y D A N P E E T
X I U K E B N Q N H O N D Y G R G Z F D
B O G J W D R M A L V H D O G I N Z L G
S W Q L O C S P B B B E D O T T B A E F
B O F Y L L A A D A S A N H W R R P C F
U L K L F N C P Q T L D O S X A I J T D
R V C W R K Q M T M S K S I M N D J I Y
I E J H B U W R I A W C F L N S E Q O C
A S X R I R G N W C I I E G S Y S J N Q
L P D N M L G Y S K C N R N A L I T T A
G Q C D H K D N N U Q G A E C V L S X K
C Y P T Q T R Q R T Y T T W H A U P V Y
F A P X L K W C G F W Z U S F N M T S P
Q C R R R D H O S T H C C W R I I C M X
G K Q F R R Q Q L J O P W I L A R V V V
P P L A A G G L X S D M S P K L R W K F
B R W H J X G H T G L E B J G J O J W H
W E Z K O O B E T O N K R S T W R M R G
S D M K L V D L V Y H H P N T D S M V B
V N A W L H R S T Z G A L X L O R J P D
P R S H M S T I R H D R B X U D N I B Z
W L T V T A K N F Q R K Y P C L U E N K
H R E A K D O G B O X E S I Y J M S S K
A N R E T S E W H S T R E N G T H J T P
```

ATTILA	CHILD	HEAD	NOSFERATU	SUNRISE
BACK	CRUCIFIX	HELSING	NOTEBOOK	THREE
BAT	DOG	HOLMWOOD	PIN	TIGER
BITE	DRINK	HOST	QUINCY	TOMBSTONES
BLOOD	DUST	LIVES	RATS	TRANSYLVANIA
BOXES	ENGLISH	LUCY	REFLECTION	VAMPIRE
BRIDES	EVIL	MASTER	SEWARD	VARNA
BURIAL	FLOWERS	MINA	SOULS	WESTERNA
CAPTAIN	GODALMING	MIND	STAKE	WINDOW
CARFAX	HARKER	MIRRORS	STRENGTH	WOLVES

Dracula Word Search 4 Answer Key

ATTILA	CHILD	HEAD	NOSFERATU	SUNRISE
BACK	CRUCIFIX	HELSING	NOTEBOOK	THREE
BAT	DOG	HOLMWOOD	PIN	TIGER
BITE	DRINK	HOST	QUINCY	TOMBSTONES
BLOOD	DUST	LIVES	RATS	TRANSYLVANIA
BOXES	ENGLISH	LUCY	REFLECTION	VAMPIRE
BRIDES	EVIL	MASTER	SEWARD	VARNA
BURIAL	FLOWERS	MINA	SOULS	WESTERNA
CAPTAIN	GODALMING	MIND	STAKE	WINDOW
CARFAX	HARKER	MIRRORS	STRENGTH	WOLVES

Dracula Crossword 1

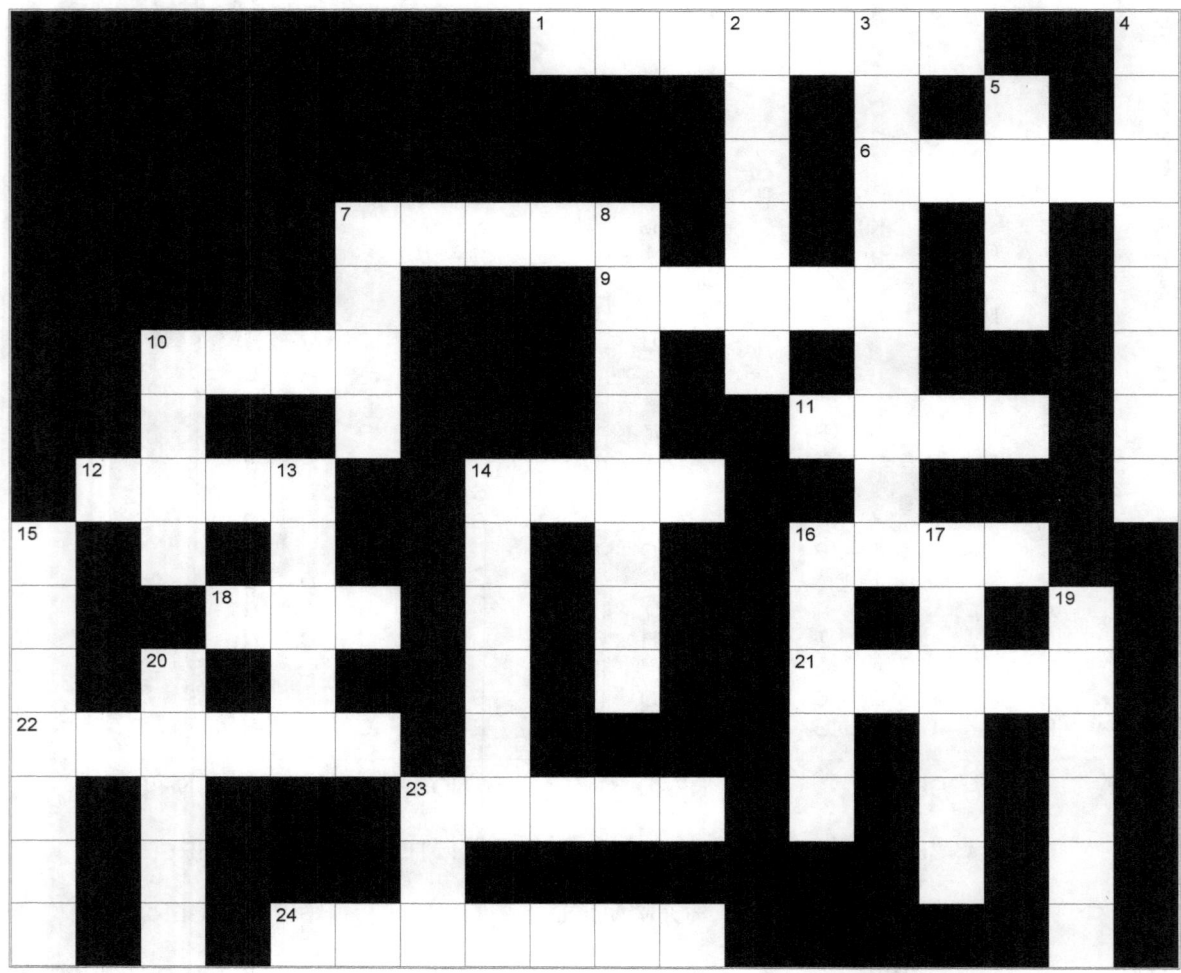

Across
1. He suggests that Lucy needs blood transfusions: Van ___
6. Renfield wants life from other beings, not ___.
7. The Slovaks deliver large, wooden ___ with rope handles to the castle.
9. Number of letters the Count instructs Jonathan to write home
10. Communion wafer used as a weapon against vampires
11. Renfield's is broken.
12. Dracula promises Renfield the lives of ____.
14. The Count's is linked to Mina's.
16. She received 3 marriage proposals in one day.
18. Mina saw one flitting in the moonlight.
21. Home port of the Demeter
22. Children of the Night
23. Renfield stops himself before uttering this word.
24. The Count wants Jonathan to teach him this.

Down
2. Van Helsing instructs him to sit with Lucy through the night without leaving her.
3. The Un-Dead
4. Lucy's mother: Mrs. ____
5. The purified vampires turn to this.
7. These marks were found on the childrens' throats.
8. Jonathan marvels at the caleche driver's
10. Van Helsing wants to cut off Lucy's ___ and take out her heart.
13. One is driven through Lucy's heart.
14. Renfield's name for the Count
15. Mrs. Westerna throws away Lucy's garlic ___.
16. Renfield collects them.
17. Dracula owns ___, which is next door to Dr. Seward's place.
19. He travels to Castle Dracula to meet with the Count about real estate.
20. Renfield laps the Doctor's off of the floor like a dog.
23. A large one jumps off the ship and disappears in the dark.

Dracula Crossword 1 Answer Key

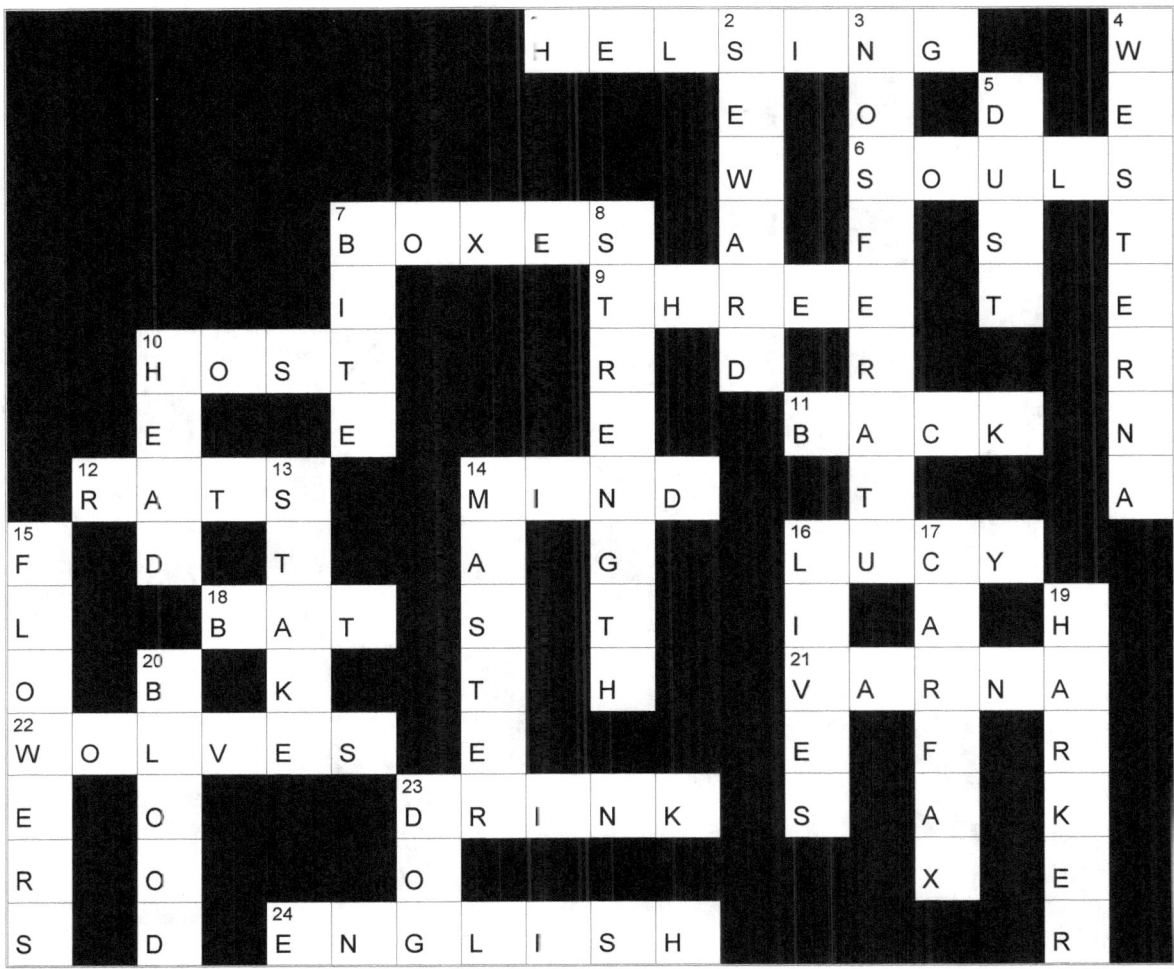

Across

1. He suggests that Lucy needs blood transfusions: Van ___
6. Renfield wants life from other beings, not ___.
7. The Slovaks deliver large, wooden ___ with rope handles to the castle.
9. Number of letters the Count instructs Jonathan to write home
10. Communion wafer used as a weapon against vampires
11. Renfield's is broken.
12. Dracula promises Renfield the lives of ____.
14. The Count's is linked to Mina's.
16. She received 3 marriage proposals in one day.
18. Mina saw one flitting in the moonlight.
21. Home port of the Demeter
22. Children of the Night
23. Renfield stops himself before uttering this word.
24. The Count wants Jonathan to teach him this.

Down

2. Van Helsing instructs him to sit with Lucy through the night without leaving her.
3. The Un-Dead
4. Lucy's mother: Mrs. ____
5. The purified vampires turn to this.
7. These marks were found on the childrens' throats.
8. Jonathan marvels at the caleche driver's
10. Van Helsing wants to cut off Lucy's ___ and take out her heart.
13. One is driven through Lucy's heart.
14. Renfield's name for the Count
15. Mrs. Westerna throws away Lucy's garlic ___.
16. Renfield collects them.
17. Dracula owns ___, which is next door to Dr. Seward's place.
19. He travels to Castle Dracula to meet with the Count about real estate.
20. Renfield laps the Doctor's off of the floor like a dog.
23. A large one jumps off the ship and disappears in the dark.

Dracula Crossword 2

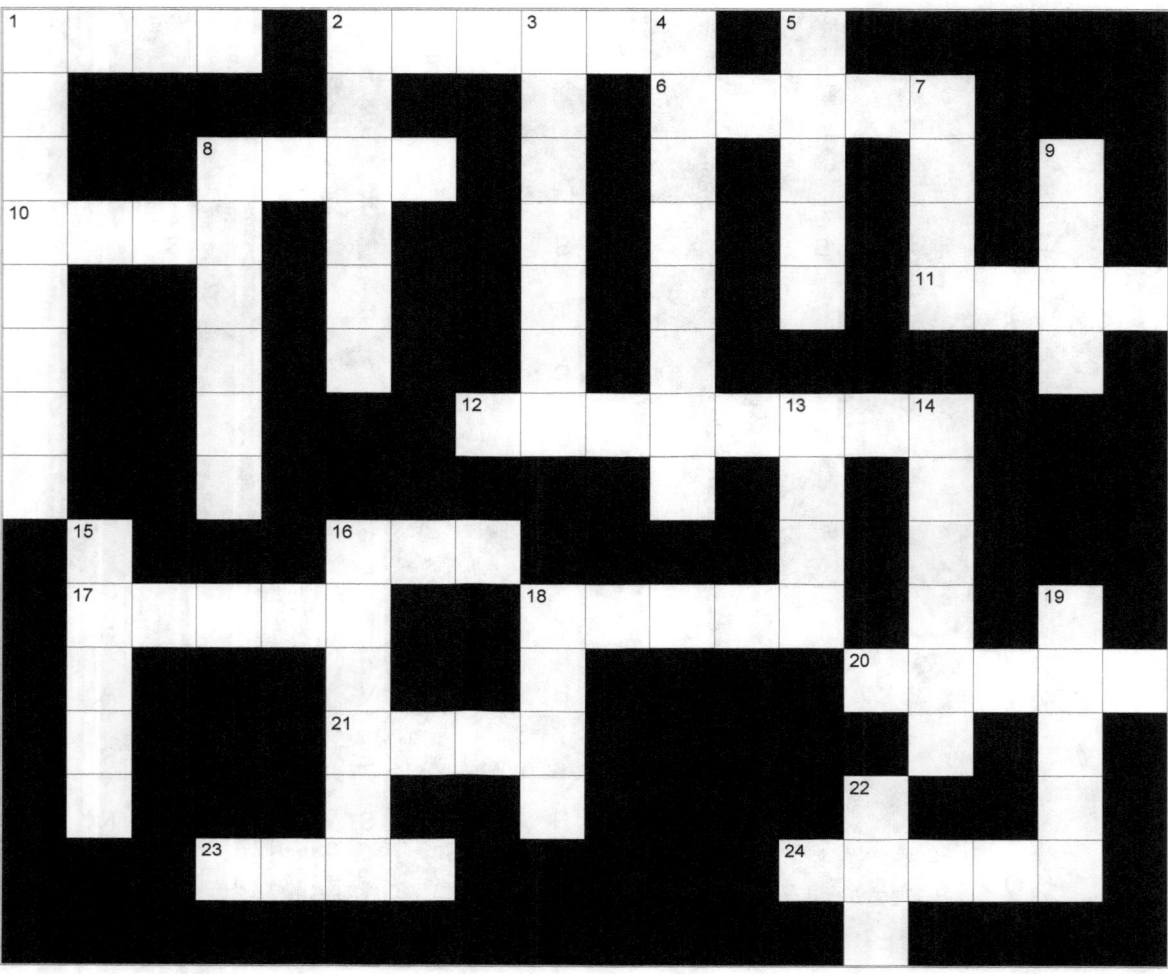

Across
1. Van Helsing wants to cut off Lucy's ___ and take out her heart.
2. Children of the Night
6. Number of letters the Count instructs Jonathan to write home
8. The Count's is linked to Mina's.
10. She is engaged to marry Jonathan.
11. She received 3 marriage proposals in one day.
12. Lucy's mother: Mrs. ____
16. Mina saw one flitting in the moonlight.
17. Van Helsing compares Dracula to one.
18. The Slovaks deliver large, wooden ___ with rope handles to the castle.
20. Renfield laps the Doctor's off of the floor like a dog.
21. The purified vampires turn to this.
23. Communion wafer used as a weapon against vampires
24. Renfield collects them.

Down
1. Lucy accepts his marriage proposal.
2. The Count escapes capture at Piccadilly by jumping our of this.
3. Dracula or Lucy, for example
4. Jonathan marvels at the caleche driver's
5. Renfield stops himself before uttering this word.
7. At midnight on St. George's Day all ___ things in the world have full sway.
8. Renfield's name for the Count
9. Renfield's is broken.
13. Dracula promises Renfield the lives of ____.
14. Count Dracula claims to be a descendant of ___ the Hun.
15. One is driven through Lucy's heart.
16. The Three voluptuous women are the ___ of Dracula.
18. These marks were found on the childrens' throats.
19. Renfield wants life from other beings, not ___.
22. Mina thinks she accidentally pricked Lucy with one.

Dracula Crossword 2 Answer Key

Across
1. Van Helsing wants to cut off Lucy's ___ and take out her heart.
2. Children of the Night
6. Number of letters the Count instructs Jonathan to write home
8. The Count's is linked to Mina's.
10. She is engaged to marry Jonathan.
11. She received 3 marriage proposals in one day.
12. Lucy's mother: Mrs. ____
16. Mina saw one flitting in the moonlight.
17. Van Helsing compares Dracula to one.
18. The Slovaks deliver large, wooden ___ with rope handles to the castle.
20. Renfield laps the Doctor's off of the floor like a dog.
21. The purified vampires turn to this.
23. Communion wafer used as a weapon against vampires
24. Renfield collects them.

Down
1. Lucy accepts his marriage proposal.
2. The Count escapes capture at Piccadilly by jumping our of this.
3. Dracula or Lucy, for example
4. Jonathan marvels at the caleche driver's
5. Renfield stops himself before uttering this word.
7. At midnight on St. George's Day all ___ things in the world have full sway.
8. Renfield's name for the Count
9. Renfield's is broken.
13. Dracula promises Renfield the lives of ____.
14. Count Dracula claims to be a descendant of ___ the Hun.
15. One is driven through Lucy's heart.
16. The Three voluptuous women are the ___ of Dracula.
18. These marks were found on the childrens' throats.
19. Renfield wants life from other beings, not ___.
22. Mina thinks she accidentally pricked Lucy with one.

Dracula Crossword 3

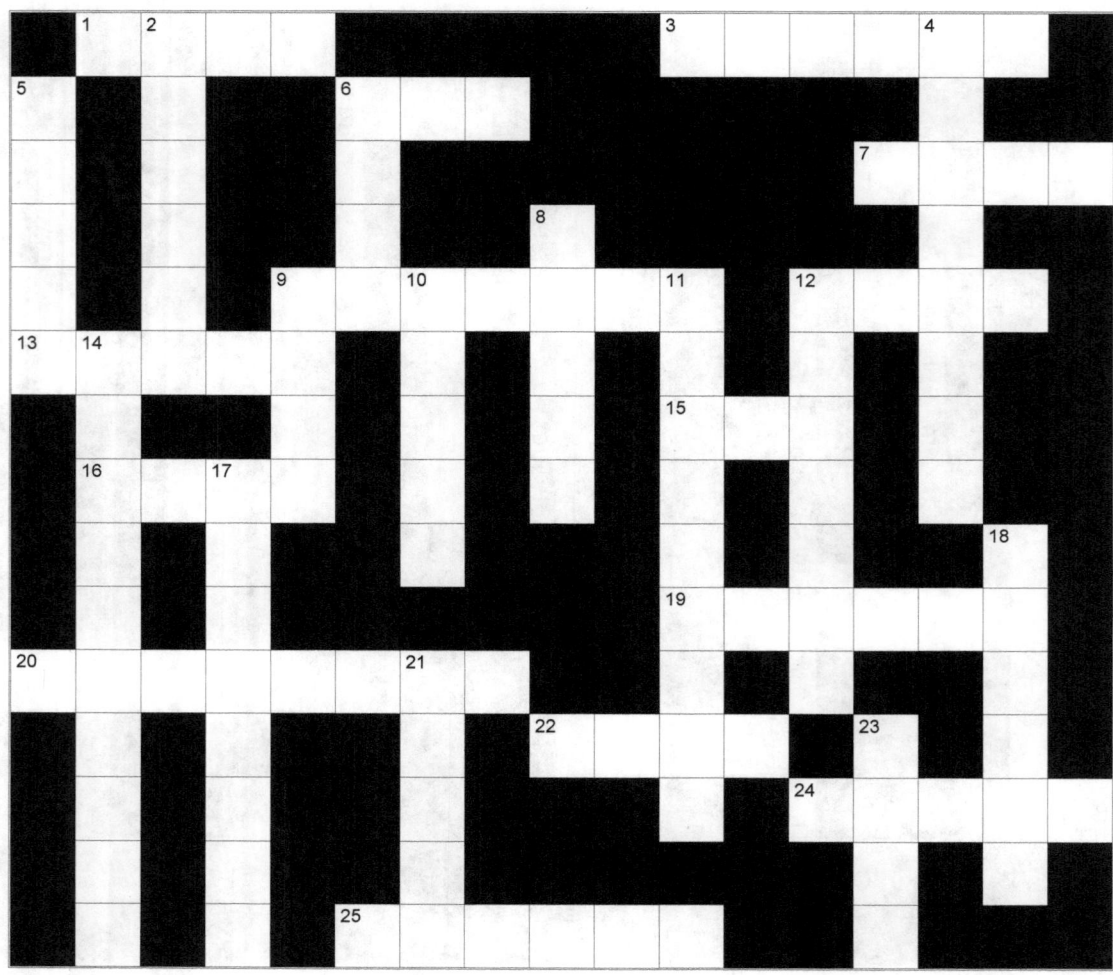

Across
1. Renfield's is broken.
3. American friend of Arthur Holmwood
6. Mina saw one flitting in the moonlight.
7. The purified vampires turn to this.
9. He suggests that Lucy needs blood transfusions: Van ___
12. At midnight on St. George's Day all ___ things in the world have full sway.
13. One is driven through Lucy's heart.
15. A large one jumps off the ship and disappears in the dark.
16. The Count's is linked to Mina's.
19. Renfield's name for the Count
20. Jonathan marvels at the caleche driver's
22. She is engaged to marry Jonathan.
24. The Slovaks deliver large, wooden ___ with rope handles to the castle.
25. Van Helsing instructs him to sit with Lucy through the night without leaving her.

Down
2. Count Dracula claims to be a descendant of ___ the Hun.
4. Hotel landlady gives Jonathan this for protection
5. Renfield wants life from other beings, not ___.
6. These marks were found on the childrens' throats.
8. Van Helsing compares Dracula to one.
9. Van Helsing wants to cut off Lucy's ___ and take out her heart.
10. Renfield collects them.
11. Arthur Holmwood: Lord ___
12. The Count wants Jonathan to teach him this.
14. The old man claims these in the graveyard lie.
17. Mina promises not to tell Jonathan about the contents of his ___ unless it becomes necessary.
18. The Three voluptuous women are the ___ of Dracula.
21. Number of letters the Count instructs Jonathan to write home
23. Communion wafer used as a weapon against vampires

Dracula Crossword 3 Answer Key

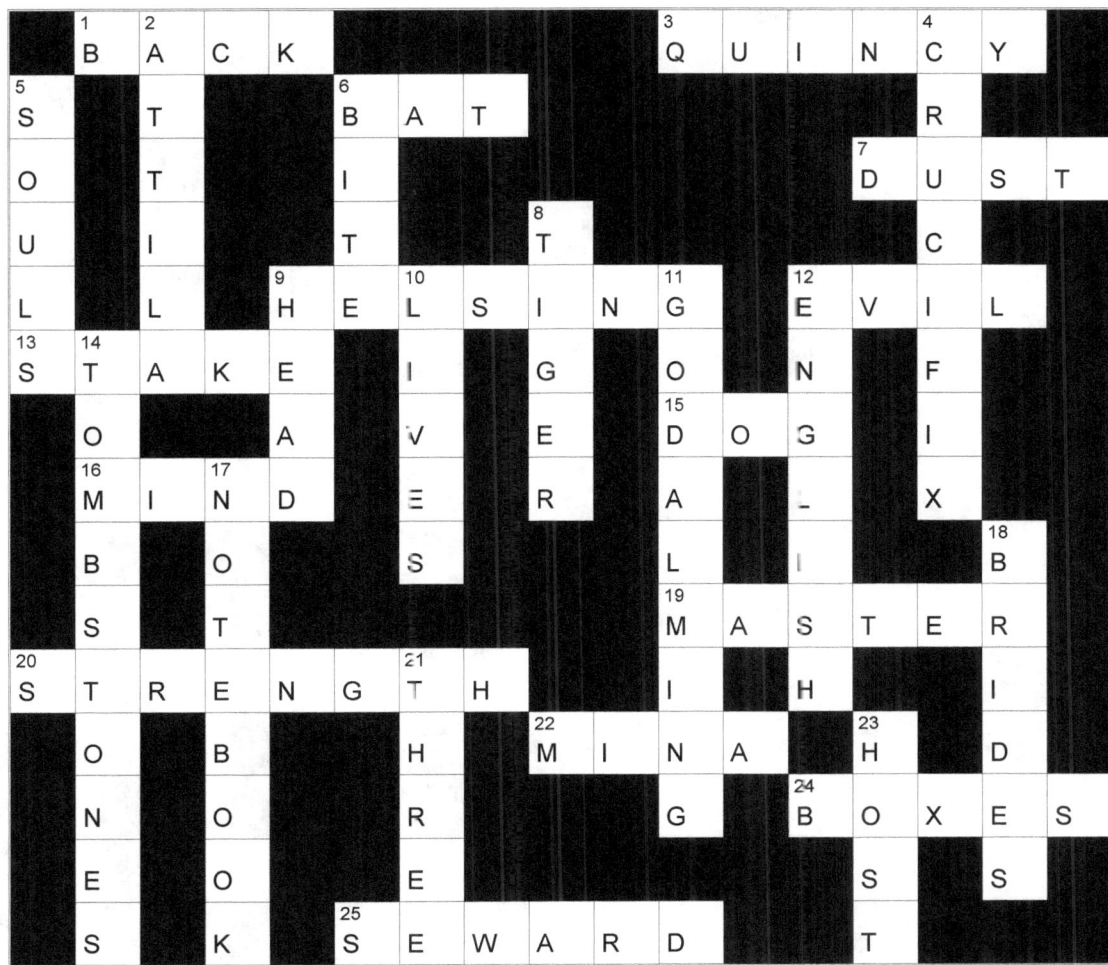

Across
1. Renfield's is broken.
3. American friend of Arthur Holmwood
6. Mina saw one flitting in the moonlight.
7. The purified vampires turn to this.
9. He suggests that Lucy needs blood transfusions: Van ___
12. At midnight on St. George's Day all ___ things in the world have full sway.
13. One is driven through Lucy's heart.
15. A large one jumps off the ship and disappears in the dark.
16. The Count's is linked to Mina's.
19. Renfield's name for the Count
20. Jonathan marvels at the caleche driver's
22. She is engaged to marry Jonathan.
24. The Slovaks deliver large, wooden ___ with rope handles to the castle.
25. Van Helsing instructs him to sit with Lucy through the night without leaving her.

Down
2. Count Dracula claims to be a descendant of ___ the Hun.
4. Hotel landlady gives Jonathan this for protection
5. Renfield wants life from other beings, not ___.
6. These marks were found on the childrens' throats.
8. Van Helsing compares Dracula to one.
9. Van Helsing wants to cut off Lucy's ___ and take out her heart.
10. Renfield collects them.
11. Arthur Holmwood: Lord ___
12. The Count wants Jonathan to teach him this.
14. The old man claims these in the graveyard lie.
17. Mina promises not to tell Jonathan about the contents of his ___ unless it becomes necessary.
18. The Three voluptuous women are the ___ of Dracula.
21. Number of letters the Count instructs Jonathan to write home
23. Communion wafer used as a weapon against vampires

Dracula Crossword 4

Across

3. The Count wants Jonathan to teach him this.
6. Dracula or Lucy, for example
8. Renfield is quiet from moonrise to ___.
10. These marks were found on the childrens' throats.
12. The Count's is linked to Mina's.
14. Mina promises not to tell Jonathan about the contents of his ___ unless it becomes necessary.
15. The purified vampires turn to this.
16. A large one jumps off the ship and disappears in the dark.
17. One is driven through Lucy's heart.
18. Renfield's is broken.
20. Van Helsing compares Dracula to one.
21. Dracula promises Renfield the lives of ____.
22. Renfield collects them.
23. The Three voluptuous women are the ___ of Dracula.
24. She received 3 marriage proposals in one day.

Down

1. Lucy's mother: Mrs. ____
2. Mina thinks she accidentally pricked Lucy with one.
4. Arthur Holmwood: Lord ____
5. Communion wafer used as a weapon against vampires
7. She is engaged to marry Jonathan.
8. Jonathan marvels at the caleche driver's
9. At midnight on St. George's Day all ___ things in the world have full sway.
10. Renfield laps the Doctor's off of the floor like a dog.
11. Children of the Night
13. Renfield stops himself before uttering this word.
14. The Un-Dead
18. The Slovaks deliver large, wooden ___ with rope handles to the castle.
19. Dracula owns ___, which is next door to Dr. Seward's place.
20. Number of letters the Count instructs Jonathan to write home

Dracula Crossword 4 Answer Key

Across
3. The Count wants Jonathan to teach him this.
6. Dracula or Lucy, for example
8. Renfield is quiet from moonrise to ___.
10. These marks were found on the childrens' throats.
12. The Count's is linked to Mina's.
14. Mina promises not to tell Jonathan about the contents of his ___ unless it becomes necessary.
15. The purified vampires turn to this.
16. A large one jumps off the ship and disappears in the dark.
17. One is driven through Lucy's heart.
18. Renfield's is broken.
20. Van Helsing compares Dracula to one.
21. Dracula promises Renfield the lives of ____.
22. Renfield collects them.
23. The Three voluptuous women are the ___ of Dracula.
24. She received 3 marriage proposals in one day.

Down
1. Lucy's mother: Mrs. ____
2. Mina thinks she accidentally pricked Lucy with one.
4. Arthur Holmwood: Lord ____
5. Communion wafer used as a weapon against vampires
7. She is engaged to marry Jonathan.
8. Jonathan marvels at the caleche driver's
9. At midnight on St. George's Day all ___ things in the world have full sway.
10. Renfield laps the Doctor's off of the floor like a dog.
11. Children of the Night
13. Renfield stops himself before uttering this word.
14. The Un-Dead
18. The Slovaks deliver large, wooden ___ with rope handles to the castle.
19. Dracula owns ___, which is next door to Dr. Seward's place.
20. Number of letters the Count instructs Jonathan to write home

Dracula

CARFAX	CRUCIFIX	HEAD	EVIL	WESTERNA
DOG	MIRRORS	WINDOW	MINA	STAKE
HELSING	WOLVES	FREE SPACE	BAT	VAMPIRE
FLOWERS	REFLECTION	MIND	TOMBSTONES	PIN
HOLMWOOD	BACK	BOXES	RATS	ENGLISH

Dracula

DUST	NOTEBOOK	LUCY	BLOOD	SEWARD
QUINCY	THREE	STRENGTH	GODALMING	TIGER
SOULS	LIVES	FREE SPACE	MASTER	NOSFERATU
ATTILA	BURIAL	CHILD	HARKER	HOST
VARNA	BITE	CAPTAIN	DRINK	SUNRISE

Dracula

PIN	VARNA	SUNRISE	STAKE	HOLMWOOD
BACK	LUCY	MIRRORS	DRINK	CARFAX
DOG	GODALMING	FREE SPACE	WINDOW	BURIAL
MASTER	TOMBSTONES	NOTEBOOK	VAMPIRE	CHILD
MIND	HEAD	LIVES	CRUCIFIX	EVIL

Dracula

TRANSYLVANIA	SOULS	ENGLISH	SEWARD	RATS
BRIDES	ATTILA	BITE	BLOOD	DUST
BOXES	QUINCY	FREE SPACE	WESTERNA	FLOWERS
HARKER	HELSING	TIGER	STRENGTH	NOSFERATU
HOST	REFLECTION	WOLVES	MINA	CAPTAIN

Dracula

BACK	WESTERNA	SUNRISE	PIN	HOST
RATS	CRUCIFIX	BLOOD	TRANSYLVANIA	BURIAL
HOLMWOOD	LIVES	FREE SPACE	MINA	HELSING
CAPTAIN	SOULS	GODALMING	NOSFERATU	QUINCY
VARNA	STRENGTH	DRINK	WINDOW	STAKE

Dracula

HEAD	TOMBSTONES	NOTEBOOK	BRIDES	HARKER
DUST	THREE	BAT	SEWARD	EVIL
DOG	VAMPIRE	FREE SPACE	LUCY	CHILD
TIGER	MIRRORS	ATTILA	BITE	MASTER
REFLECTION	MIND	CARFAX	WOLVES	ENGLISH

Dracula

WESTERNA	MIND	VARNA	CAPTAIN	DOG
NOTEBOOK	DUST	QUINCY	HEAD	FLOWERS
GODALMING	BITE	FREE SPACE	LUCY	STAKE
HOST	HELSING	TOMBSTONES	EVIL	REFLECTION
CHILD	WINDOW	BAT	SUNRISE	BLOOD

Dracula

TIGER	BACK	BOXES	LIVES	VAMPIRE
ATTILA	BURIAL	RATS	THREE	MASTER
SEWARD	WOLVES	FREE SPACE	HOLMWOOD	NOSFERATU
BRIDES	CARFAX	CRUCIFIX	STRENGTH	DRINK
MIRRORS	HARKER	SOULS	PIN	TRANSYLVANIA

Dracula

BLOOD	THREE	RATS	WINDOW	TOMBSTONES
BURIAL	BITE	QUINCY	REFLECTION	DRINK
NOTEBOOK	TIGER	FREE SPACE	VARNA	BAT
HARKER	BACK	HOLMWOOD	ENGLISH	SEWARD
ATTILA	SUNRISE	STAKE	EVIL	SOULS

Dracula

DUST	WESTERNA	TRANSYLVANIA	BOXES	MIND
VAMPIRE	HELSING	LUCY	MASTER	PIN
LIVES	CAPTAIN	FREE SPACE	STRENGTH	WOLVES
GODALMING	MINA	CHILD	BRIDES	DOG
CARFAX	MIRRORS	HOST	NOSFERATU	CRUCIFIX

Dracula

BAT	MIND	DUST	SUNRISE	NOTEBOOK
BURIAL	FLOWERS	CHILD	MIRRORS	NOSFERATU
BRIDES	REFLECTION	FREE SPACE	TRANSYLVANIA	STRENGTH
WESTERNA	VAMPIRE	SEWARD	BACK	STAKE
RATS	BLOOD	PIN	ENGLISH	HELSING

Dracula

DOG	HOLMWOOD	ATTILA	TOMBSTONES	MINA
DRINK	LIVES	BOXES	THREE	WINDOW
CAPTAIN	HEAD	FREE SPACE	WOLVES	LUCY
SOULS	HARKER	TIGER	HOST	VARNA
GODALMING	EVIL	BITE	CRUCIFIX	CARFAX

Dracula

HOST	DUST	CARFAX	TIGER	VARNA
BURIAL	VAMPIRE	TRANSYLVANIA	QUINCY	DRINK
BACK	BITE	FREE SPACE	BLOOD	CAPTAIN
THREE	HOLMWOOD	BOXES	ENGLISH	NOTEBOOK
CHILD	RATS	STRENGTH	STAKE	SEWARD

Dracula

BAT	BRIDES	CRUCIFIX	MINA	WINDOW
PIN	FLOWERS	HARKER	WESTERNA	EVIL
REFLECTION	LIVES	FREE SPACE	GODALMING	SUNRISE
MIRRORS	HEAD	HELSING	DOG	WOLVES
MIND	ATTILA	SOULS	NOSFERATU	LUCY

Dracula

DOG	TIGER	QUINCY	BOXES	MIND
STRENGTH	CRUCIFIX	NOTEBOOK	HELSING	STAKE
WOLVES	HOLMWOOD	FREE SPACE	MASTER	PIN
SOULS	TRANSYLVANIA	LUCY	CHILD	CARFAX
SEWARD	THREE	GODALMING	NOSFERATU	EVIL

Dracula

CAPTAIN	WINDOW	VAMPIRE	BACK	BURIAL
BAT	HEAD	FLOWERS	VARNA	SUNRISE
HOST	TOMBSTONES	FREE SPACE	LIVES	DRINK
BLOOD	MINA	BITE	WESTERNA	ATTILA
ENGLISH	MIRRORS	RATS	HARKER	DUST

Dracula

REFLECTION	TOMBSTONES	NOTEBOOK	LIVES	THREE
ENGLISH	BLOOD	WINDOW	RATS	VAMPIRE
STRENGTH	QUINCY	FREE SPACE	HARKER	STAKE
BRIDES	EVIL	SOULS	BURIAL	VARNA
SEWARD	HEAD	MINA	LUCY	DRINK

Dracula

CARFAX	BITE	DOG	HELSING	MIND
TIGER	WESTERNA	CHILD	DUST	PIN
WOLVES	ATTILA	FREE SPACE	TRANSYLVANIA	BAT
GODALMING	MIRRORS	FLOWERS	NOSFERATU	BACK
HOST	CRUCIFIX	SUNRISE	MASTER	BOXES

Dracula

REFLECTION	STRENGTH	EVIL	BOXES	TOMBSTONES
THREE	TIGER	HARKER	CHILD	VAMPIRE
BRIDES	CAPTAIN	FREE SPACE	HOLMWOOD	FLOWERS
NOSFERATU	LUCY	PIN	LIVES	ATTILA
MIRRORS	MASTER	SOULS	ENGLISH	MINA

Dracula

BURIAL	BAT	DOG	HEAD	BITE
MIND	WESTERNA	WOLVES	CARFAX	SUNRISE
BACK	SEWARD	FREE SPACE	WINDOW	DRINK
BLOOD	RATS	DUST	NOTEBOOK	CRUCIFIX
QUINCY	HELSING	STAKE	TRANSYLVANIA	GODALMING

Dracula

WINDOW	DRINK	RATS	WESTERNA	STRENGTH
BLOOD	ENGLISH	VARNA	SUNRISE	MIND
DOG	NOTEBOOK	FREE SPACE	HARKER	TOMBSTONES
SOULS	CHILD	CARFAX	FLOWERS	THREE
CAPTAIN	NOSFERATU	BAT	HEAD	BACK

Dracula

PIN	MIRRORS	ATTILA	SEWARD	HOLMWOOD
BOXES	BRIDES	LIVES	HELSING	DUST
GODALMING	BURIAL	FREE SPACE	QUINCY	VAMPIRE
HOST	TRANSYLVANIA	MINA	REFLECTION	LUCY
MASTER	BITE	EVIL	STAKE	CRUCIFIX

Dracula

TIGER	ATTILA	QUINCY	GODALMING	MIRRORS
SOULS	HELSING	THREE	RATS	WESTENRA
TOMBSTONES	NOTEBOOK	FREE SPACE	WOLVES	NOSFERATU
VARNA	SUNRISE	CARFAX	DOG	HOLMWOOD
HEAD	BOXES	CAPTAIN	MASTER	DRINK

Dracula

PIN	SEWARD	STAKE	BLOOD	MIND
FLOWERS	ENGLISH	BITE	TRANSYLVANIA	HOST
BURIAL	MINA	FREE SPACE	BACK	EVIL
BRIDES	BAT	WINDOW	CRUCIFIX	HARKER
DUST	VAMPIRE	STRENGTH	REFLECTION	LIVES

Dracula

MASTER	CHILD	WESTERNA	THREE	BITE
WOLVES	MIRRORS	EVIL	CAPTAIN	HEAD
DOG	HOLMWOOD	FREE SPACE	SEWARD	BRIDES
DRINK	WINDOW	LUCY	REFLECTION	TIGER
BACK	NOSFERATU	SUNRISE	MINA	CARFAX

Dracula

MIND	BLOOD	SOULS	DUST	BAT
RATS	TRANSYLVANIA	PIN	STRENGTH	LIVES
CRUCIFIX	NOTEBOOK	FREE SPACE	VAMPIRE	STAKE
ATTILA	GODALMING	FLOWERS	HARKER	VARNA
HELSING	TOMBSTONES	QUINCY	BURIAL	BOXES

Dracula

ATTILA	MINA	HOLMWOOD	NOSFERATU	VAMPIRE
BRIDES	EVIL	TRANSYLVANIA	HOST	THREE
LIVES	WESTERNA	FREE SPACE	BITE	CRUCIFIX
TIGER	STRENGTH	DUST	HELSING	SEWARD
LUCY	DOG	STAKE	WINDOW	QUINCY

Dracula

PIN	BAT	SOULS	ENGLISH	CAPTAIN
TOMBSTONES	MASTER	NOTEBOOK	SUNRISE	BLOOD
BOXES	CARFAX	FREE SPACE	BACK	DRINK
VARNA	BURIAL	HEAD	RATS	WOLVES
CHILD	MIRRORS	GODALMING	REFLECTION	FLOWERS

Dracula

REFLECTION	DRINK	FLOWERS	EVIL	MIND
CAPTAIN	SEWARD	VAMPIRE	SUNRISE	WESTERNA
MINA	BAT	FREE SPACE	ENGLISH	CARFAX
HARKER	QUINCY	BITE	TOMBSTONES	VARNA
ATTILA	GODALMING	BLOOD	HEAD	BOXES

Dracula

LIVES	MASTER	LUCY	STRENGTH	DUST
SOULS	PIN	HOLMWOOD	CHILD	HELSING
NOSFERATU	THREE	FREE SPACE	MIRRORS	HOST
WINDOW	NOTEBOOK	TRANSYLVANIA	BURIAL	WOLVES
DOG	TIGER	BRIDES	CRUCIFIX	STAKE

Dracula

STRENGTH	ENGLISH	WOLVES	LUCY	PIN
BURIAL	WESTERNA	EVIL	FLOWERS	CAPTAIN
BAT	DOG	FREE SPACE	VAMPIRE	SUNRISE
CRUCIFIX	NOTEBOOK	TOMBSTONES	DRINK	LIVES
MASTER	NOSFERATU	MIND	QUINCY	TIGER

Dracula

CHILD	SEWARD	RATS	CARFAX	HELSING
BOXES	HARKER	TRANSYLVANIA	GODALMING	BACK
SOULS	BITE	FREE SPACE	DUST	THREE
BRIDES	HOLMWOOD	STAKE	MINA	HEAD
ATTILA	MIRRORS	REFLECTION	HOST	WINDOW

Dracula Vocabulary Word List

No.	Word	Clue/Definition
1.	ABASEMENT	Low or downcast state
2.	ABATED	Reduced in amount, degree, or intensity
3.	ACCENTUATED	Stressed or emphasized; intensified
4.	ACQUIESCED	Consented or complied passively or without protest
5.	ACQUIESCED	Consent or comply passively or without protest
6.	ACUMEN	Quickness, accuracy, and keenness of judgment or insight
7.	ADDENDUM	Something added or to be added, as in a supplement to a book
8.	ADDUCE	Cite as an example or means of proof in an argument
9.	AFFLICT	Inflict grievous physical or mental suffering on
10.	AGGLOMERATION	Confused or jumbled mass
11.	AGUE	Chill or fit of shivering
12.	ALACRITY	Cheerful willingness; eagerness; speed or quickness
13.	AMENABLE	Responsive to advice, authority, or suggestion; willing
14.	ASCERTAIN	Make certain, definite, and precise
15.	ASSAIL	Attack, as with ridicule
16.	ASSIDUOUSLY	With care and persistence
17.	ASSIMILATION	Adopting the customs and attitudes of the prevailing culture
18.	AVARICE	Immoderate desire for wealth; greed
19.	BOUDOIR	Woman's private sitting room, dressing room, or bedroom
20.	CALECHE	Light carriage with two or four low wheels and a collapsible top
21.	CHAGRIN	Strong feelings of embarrassment
22.	CONSIGNING	Giving over to the care of another
23.	CONSTRAINED	In a forced or inhibited manner
24.	CONVERGED	Came together from different directions
25.	DEBAUCH	Corrupt morally
26.	DEFERENCE	Yielding to the opinion, wishes, or judgment of another
27.	DEMURRED	Voiced opposition; objected
28.	DESPATCH	Written, official message sent with speed
29.	DIORAMA	Scene in which figures are arranged in a naturalistic setting against a painted background
30.	DISPOSITION	One's usual mood; temperament
31.	DISSIPATED	Drove away; dispersed
32.	DISTILS	Separates or purifies
33.	ELUDE	Evade or escape from, as by daring, cleverness, or skill
34.	EMACIATED	Extremely thin, especially as a result of starvation
35.	EMINENCE	Position of great distinction or superiority
36.	ENIGMATICAL	Puzzling or mysterious
37.	ENTAILED	Limited inheritance of property to specified heirs
38.	EXPOSTULATE	Reason with someone in an effort to dissuade or correct
39.	FISSURE	Long, narrow opening; a crack or cleft
40.	HAGGARD	Appearing worn and exhausted
41.	HOODWINK	Take in by deceptive means; deceive
42.	HUSBANDRY	Practice of growing crops, & breeding and raising livestock
43.	IMPERTURBABLE	Unshakably calm and collected
44.	IMPLICITLY	In a manner which is understood though not directly expressed
45.	IMPOTENT	Lacking physical strength or vigor; weak
46.	IMPREGNABLE	Impossible to capture or enter by force
47.	INQUIETUDE	State of restlessness or uneasiness
48.	INQUISITION	The act of inquiring into a matter; an investigation
49.	INSTIGATION	Deliberate triggering of trouble or discord
50.	INTRIGUED	Engaged in secret or underhanded schemes; spied

Dracula Vocabulary Word List Continued

No.	Word	Clue/Definition
51.	IRKSOME	Causing annoyance, weariness, or vexation
52.	LAIR	Den or dwelling of a wild animal; a hideaway
53.	LANGUID	Lacking energy or vitality; weak
54.	MAELSTROM	Violent or turbulent situation; a large, violent whirlpool
55.	MALADY	Disease, disorder, or ailment
56.	MALIGNITY	Intense ill will or hatred; great malice
57.	MALODOROUS	Having a bad odor; foul
58.	MENIAL	Relating to work regarded as for a servant
59.	MUNDANE	Relating to commonplace things; ordinary
60.	ODIUM	Strong dislike, contempt or aversion
61.	PALLOR	Extreme or unnatural paleness
62.	PAROXYSM	Sudden outburst of emotion or action
63.	PLACIDITY	Quality of being undisturbed by tumult or disorder; relaxation
64.	POIGNANT	Distressing to the mind or feelings; profoundly moving or touching
65.	PORTERAGE	Charge for the carrying of burdens or goods as done by porters
66.	PRESAGE	Indication or warning of a future occurrence; an omen
67.	PRODIGIOUS	Impressively great in size, force, or extent; enormous
68.	PROLIFIC	Producing abundant works or results
69.	PROSAIC	Matter-of-fact; straightforward; lacking imagination; dull
70.	QUERIED	Questioned; inquired
71.	REMONSTRANCE	Expression of protest or complaint
72.	REPUDIATED	Rejected emphatically as unfounded, untrue, or unjust
73.	REQUISITIONS	Formal, written requests for something needed
74.	RESONANT	Strong and deep in tone
75.	RESUMPTION	Beginning again
76.	RETICENT	Inclined to keep one's thoughts, feelings, and personal affairs to oneself
77.	REVERENTLY	In a state of profound awe and respect and often love
78.	SANGUINE	Cheerfully confident; optimistic; of a healthy reddish color
79.	SATURNINE	Melancholy or sullen; tending to be bitter
80.	SEXTON	Employee responsible for the upkeep of church property
81.	SMOTE	Struck down or hit
82.	SOPHISTIC	Characteristic of a scholar or thinker
83.	STALWART	Having or marked by imposing physical strength
84.	SUCCUMBED	Yielded to an overwhelming desire; gave up or gave in
85.	TACIT	Not spoken
86.	TETHER	Restrain for holding an animal in place
87.	THWARTING	Opposing and defeating the efforts, plans, or ambitions of something
88.	TORRENT	Heavy, uncontrolled outpouring
89.	TRENCHANT	Forceful, effective, and vigorous
90.	TUMULT	Agitation of the mind or emotions
91.	UNFETTERED	Set free or kept free from restrictions or bonds
92.	UNHALLOWED	Unholy
93.	URBANE	Polite, refined, and often elegant in manner
94.	VERBATIM	In exactly the same words; word for word
95.	VIADUCT	Bridge consisting of arches used to carry a road over a valley
96.	VOLUPTUOUS	Arising from or contributing to the satisfaction of sensual desires
97.	WILY	Marked by skill in deception

Dracula Vocabulary Fill in the Blanks 1

_____ 1. Adopting the customs and attitudes of the prevailing culture

_____ 2. Struck down or hit

_____ 3. Having a bad odor; foul

_____ 4. Engaged in secret or underhanded schemes; spied

_____ 5. Something added or to be added, as in a supplement to a book

_____ 6. Giving over to the care of another

_____ 7. In a forced or inhibited manner

_____ 8. The act of inquiring into a matter; an investigation

_____ 9. Yielding to the opinion, wishes, or judgment of another

_____ 10. Beginning again

_____ 11. Reason with someone in an effort to dissuade or correct

_____ 12. Low or downcast state

_____ 13. With care and persistence

_____ 14. In a manner which is understood though not directly expressed

_____ 15. Appearing worn and exhausted

_____ 16. Unholy

_____ 17. Heavy, uncontrolled outpouring

_____ 18. Den or dwelling of a wild animal; a hideaway

_____ 19. Light carriage with two or four low wheels and a collapsible top

_____ 20. Unshakably calm and collected

Dracula Vocabulary Fill in the Blanks 1 Answer Key

ASSIMILATION	1. Adopting the customs and attitudes of the prevailing culture
SMOTE	2. Struck down or hit
MALODOROUS	3. Having a bad odor; foul
INTRIGUED	4. Engaged in secret or underhanded schemes; spied
ADDENDUM	5. Something added or to be added, as in a supplement to a book
CONSIGNING	6. Giving over to the care of another
CONSTRAINED	7. In a forced or inhibited manner
INQUISITION	8. The act of inquiring into a matter; an investigation
DEFERENCE	9. Yielding to the opinion, wishes, or judgment of another
RESUMPTION	10. Beginning again
EXPOSTULATE	11. Reason with someone in an effort to dissuade or correct
ABASEMENT	12. Low or downcast state
ASSIDUOUSLY	13. With care and persistence
IMPLICITLY	14. In a manner which is understood though not directly expressed
HAGGARD	15. Appearing worn and exhausted
UNHALLOWED	16. Unholy
TORRENT	17. Heavy, uncontrolled outpouring
LAIR	18. Den or dwelling of a wild animal; a hideaway
CALECHE	19. Light carriage with two or four low wheels and a collapsible top
IMPERTURBABLE	20. Unshakably calm and collected

Dracula Vocabulary Fill in the Blanks 2

_____ 1. Relating to commonplace things; ordinary

_____ 2. In a manner which is understood though not directly expressed

_____ 3. Set free or kept free from restrictions or bonds

_____ 4. Practice of growing crops, & breeding and raising livestock

_____ 5. Woman's private sitting room, dressing room, or bedroom

_____ 6. Quickness, accuracy, and keenness of judgment or insight

_____ 7. Scene in which figures are arranged in a naturalistic setting against a painted background

_____ 8. Came together from different directions

_____ 9. Consent or comply passively or without protest

_____ 10. Extremely thin, especially as a result of starvation

_____ 11. Extreme or unnatural paleness

_____ 12. Indication or warning of a future occurrence; an omen

_____ 13. Corrupt morally

_____ 14. Den or dwelling of a wild animal; a hideaway

_____ 15. Inflict grievous physical or mental suffering on

_____ 16. Distressing to the mind or feelings; profoundly moving or touching

_____ 17. Agitation of the mind or emotions

_____ 18. Lacking physical strength or vigor; weak

_____ 19. Take in by deceptive means; deceive

_____ 20. Low or downcast state

Dracula Vocabulary Fill in the Blanks 2 Answer Key

MUNDANE	1. Relating to commonplace things; ordinary
IMPLICITLY	2. In a manner which is understood though not directly expressed
UNFETTERED	3. Set free or kept free from restrictions or bonds
HUSBANDRY	4. Practice of growing crops, & breeding and raising livestock
BOUDOIR	5. Woman's private sitting room, dressing room, or bedroom
ACUMEN	6. Quickness, accuracy, and keenness of judgment or insight
DIORAMA	7. Scene in which figures are arranged in a naturalistic setting against a painted background
CONVERGED	8. Came together from different directions
ACQUIESCED	9. Consent or comply passively or without protest
EMACIATED	10. Extremely thin, especially as a result of starvation
PALLOR	11. Extreme or unnatural paleness
PRESAGE	12. Indication or warning of a future occurrence; an omen
DEBAUCH	13. Corrupt morally
LAIR	14. Den or dwelling of a wild animal; a hideaway
AFFLICT	15. Inflict grievous physical or mental suffering on
POIGNANT	16. Distressing to the mind or feelings; profoundly moving or touching
TUMULT	17. Agitation of the mind or emotions
IMPOTENT	18. Lacking physical strength or vigor; weak
HOODWINK	19. Take in by deceptive means; deceive
ABASEMENT	20. Low or downcast state

Dracula Vocabulary Fill in the Blanks 3

_____ 1. Yielding to the opinion, wishes, or judgment of another

_____ 2. Having or marked by imposing physical strength

_____ 3. Drove away; dispersed

_____ 4. Having a bad odor; foul

_____ 5. Beginning again

_____ 6. Voiced opposition; objected

_____ 7. Woman's private sitting room, dressing room, or bedroom

_____ 8. Giving over to the care of another

_____ 9. Appearing worn and exhausted

_____ 10. Take in by deceptive means; deceive

_____ 11. Agitation of the mind or emotions

_____ 12. Impossible to capture or enter by force

_____ 13. Relating to work regarded as for a servant

_____ 14. One's usual mood; temperament

_____ 15. Stressed or emphasized; intensified

_____ 16. Came together from different directions

_____ 17. Melancholy or sullen; tending to be bitter

_____ 18. The act of inquiring into a matter; an investigation

_____ 19. Inclined to keep one's thoughts, feelings, and personal affairs to oneself

_____ 20. Employee responsible for the upkeep of church property

Dracula Vocabulary Fill in the Blanks 3 Answer Key

DEFERENCE	1. Yielding to the opinion, wishes, or judgment of another
STALWART	2. Having or marked by imposing physical strength
DISSIPATED	3. Drove away; dispersed
MALODOROUS	4. Having a bad odor; foul
RESUMPTION	5. Beginning again
DEMURRED	6. Voiced opposition; objected
BOUDOIR	7. Woman's private sitting room, dressing room, or bedroom
CONSIGNING	8. Giving over to the care of another
HAGGARD	9. Appearing worn and exhausted
HOODWINK	10. Take in by deceptive means; deceive
TUMULT	11. Agitation of the mind or emotions
IMPREGNABLE	12. Impossible to capture or enter by force
MENIAL	13. Relating to work regarded as for a servant
DISPOSITION	14. One's usual mood; temperament
ACCENTUATED	15. Stressed or emphasized; intensified
CONVERGED	16. Came together from different directions
SATURNINE	17. Melancholy or sullen; tending to be bitter
INQUISITION	18. The act of inquiring into a matter; an investigation
RETICENT	19. Inclined to keep one's thoughts, feelings, and personal affairs to oneself
SEXTON	20. Employee responsible for the upkeep of church property

Dracula Vocabulary Fill in the Blanks 4

_____ 1. Distressing to the mind or feelings; profoundly moving or touching
_____ 2. Agitation of the mind or emotions
_____ 3. Practice of growing crops, & breeding and raising livestock
_____ 4. Bridge consisting of arches used to carry a road over a valley
_____ 5. Separates or purifies
_____ 6. Drove away; dispersed
_____ 7. Impossible to capture or enter by force
_____ 8. Unholy
_____ 9. Strong feelings of embarrassment
_____ 10. Reason with someone in an effort to dissuade or correct
_____ 11. Reduced in amount, degree, or intensity
_____ 12. Polite, refined, and often elegant in manner
_____ 13. Characteristic of a scholar or thinker
_____ 14. Marked by skill in deception
_____ 15. Lacking energy or vitality; weak
_____ 16. Make certain, definite, and precise
_____ 17. In a forced or inhibited manner
_____ 18. Impressively great in size, force, or extent; enormous
_____ 19. Evade or escape from, as by daring, cleverness, or skill
_____ 20. Limited inheritance of property to specified heirs

Dracula Vocabulary Fill in the Blanks 4 Answer Key

POIGNANT	1. Distressing to the mind or feelings; profoundly moving or touching
TUMULT	2. Agitation of the mind or emotions
HUSBANDRY	3. Practice of growing crops, & breeding and raising livestock
VIADUCT	4. Bridge consisting of arches used to carry a road over a valley
DISTILS	5. Separates or purifies
DISSIPATED	6. Drove away; dispersed
IMPREGNABLE	7. Impossible to capture or enter by force
UNHALLOWED	8. Unholy
CHAGRIN	9. Strong feelings of embarrassment
EXPOSTULATE	10. Reason with someone in an effort to dissuade or correct
ABATED	11. Reduced in amount, degree, or intensity
URBANE	12. Polite, refined, and often elegant in manner
SOPHISTIC	13. Characteristic of a scholar or thinker
WILY	14. Marked by skill in deception
LANGUID	15. Lacking energy or vitality; weak
ASCERTAIN	16. Make certain, definite, and precise
CONSTRAINED	17. In a forced or inhibited manner
PRODIGIOUS	18. Impressively great in size, force, or extent; enormous
ELUDE	19. Evade or escape from, as by daring, cleverness, or skill
ENTAILED	20. Limited inheritance of property to specified heirs

Dracula Vocabulary Matching 1

___ 1. VOLUPTUOUS	A.	Having a bad odor; foul
___ 2. CONSIGNING	B.	Opposing and defeating the efforts, plans, or ambitions of something
___ 3. PALLOR	C.	Relating to commonplace things; ordinary
___ 4. VIADUCT	D.	Charge for the carrying of burdens or goods as done by porters
___ 5. SOPHISTIC	E.	Struck down or hit
___ 6. AMENABLE	F.	Consent or comply passively or without protest
___ 7. DEFERENCE	G.	Marked by skill in deception
___ 8. MUNDANE	H.	Rejected emphatically as unfounded, untrue, or unjust
___ 9. PORTERAGE	I.	Light carriage with two or four low wheels and a collapsible top
___10. QUERIED	J.	Giving over to the care of another
___11. INTRIGUED	K.	Yielding to the opinion, wishes, or judgment of another
___12. SMOTE	L.	Characteristic of a scholar or thinker
___13. PLACIDITY	M.	Arising from or contributing to the satisfaction of sensual desires
___14. FISSURE	N.	Quality of being undisturbed by tumult or disorder; relaxation
___15. MALODOROUS	O.	Limited inheritance of property to specified heirs
___16. ODIUM	P.	Extremely thin, especially as a result of starvation
___17. DEBAUCH	Q.	Responsive to advice, authority, or suggestion; willing
___18. THWARTING	R.	Engaged in secret or underhanded schemes; spied
___19. ACQUIESCED	S.	Heavy, uncontrolled outpouring
___20. TORRENT	T.	Long, narrow opening; a crack or cleft
___21. REPUDIATED	U.	Corrupt morally
___22. EMACIATED	V.	Questioned; inquired
___23. CALECHE	W.	Extreme or unnatural paleness
___24. WILY	X.	Bridge consisting of arches used to carry a road over a valley
___25. ENTAILED	Y.	Strong dislike, contempt or aversion

Dracula Vocabulary Matching 1 Answer Key

M - 1.	VOLUPTUOUS	A.	Having a bad odor; foul
J - 2.	CONSIGNING	B.	Opposing and defeating the efforts, plans, or ambitions of something
W - 3.	PALLOR	C.	Relating to commonplace things; ordinary
X - 4.	VIADUCT	D.	Charge for the carrying of burdens or goods as done by porters
L - 5.	SOPHISTIC	E.	Struck down or hit
Q - 6.	AMENABLE	F.	Consent or comply passively or without protest
K - 7.	DEFERENCE	G.	Marked by skill in deception
C - 8.	MUNDANE	H.	Rejected emphatically as unfounded, untrue, or unjust
D - 9.	PORTERAGE	I.	Light carriage with two or four low wheels and a collapsible top
V - 10.	QUERIED	J.	Giving over to the care of another
R - 11.	INTRIGUED	K.	Yielding to the opinion, wishes, or judgment of another
E - 12.	SMOTE	L.	Characteristic of a scholar or thinker
N - 13.	PLACIDITY	M.	Arising from or contributing to the satisfaction of sensual desires
T - 14.	FISSURE	N.	Quality of being undisturbed by tumult or disorder; relaxation
A - 15.	MALODOROUS	O.	Limited inheritance of property to specified heirs
Y - 16.	ODIUM	P.	Extremely thin, especially as a result of starvation
U - 17.	DEBAUCH	Q.	Responsive to advice, authority, or suggestion; willing
B - 18.	THWARTING	R.	Engaged in secret or underhanded schemes; spied
F - 19.	ACQUIESCED	S.	Heavy, uncontrolled outpouring
S - 20.	TORRENT	T.	Long, narrow opening; a crack or cleft
H - 21.	REPUDIATED	U.	Corrupt morally
P - 22.	EMACIATED	V.	Questioned; inquired
I - 23.	CALECHE	W.	Extreme or unnatural paleness
G - 24.	WILY	X.	Bridge consisting of arches used to carry a road over a valley
O - 25.	ENTAILED	Y.	Strong dislike, contempt or aversion

Dracula Vocabulary Matching 2

___ 1. CONSIGNING   A. Adopting the customs and attitudes of the prevailing culture
___ 2. ASSIDUOUSLY   B. Giving over to the care of another
___ 3. DESPATCH   C. Impressively great in size, force, or extent; enormous
___ 4. ACQUIESCED   D. Formal, written requests for something needed
___ 5. RETICENT   E. Reason with someone in an effort to dissuade or correct
___ 6. ASSIMILATION   F. Charge for the carrying of burdens or goods as done by porters
___ 7. DISTILS   G. Questioned; inquired
___ 8. PRODIGIOUS   H. Struck down or hit
___ 9. AGUE   I. Reduced in amount, degree, or intensity
___10. ABATED   J. Written, official message sent with speed
___11. MALODOROUS   K. Chill or fit of shivering
___12. AFFLICT   L. With care and persistence
___13. PORTERAGE   M. Inflict grievous physical or mental suffering on
___14. VERBATIM   N. Polite, refined, and often elegant in manner
___15. URBANE   O. Causing annoyance, weariness, or vexation
___16. ALACRITY   P. Cheerful willingness; eagerness; speed or quickness
___17. IRKSOME   Q. In exactly the same words; word for word
___18. EXPOSTULATE   R. Scene in which figures are arranged in a naturalistic setting against a painted background
___19. SUCCUMBED   S. Heavy, uncontrolled outpouring
___20. IMPREGNABLE   T. Consented or complied passively or without protest
___21. QUERIED   U. Separates or purifies
___22. REQUISITIONS   V. Impossible to capture or enter by force
___23. TORRENT   W. Inclined to keep one's thoughts, feelings, and personal affairs to oneself
___24. SMOTE   X. Having a bad odor; foul
___25. DIORAMA   Y. Yielded to an overwhelming desire; gave up or gave in

Dracula Vocabulary Matching 2 Answer Key

B - 1. CONSIGNING	A.	Adopting the customs and attitudes of the prevailing culture
L - 2. ASSIDUOUSLY	B.	Giving over to the care of another
J - 3. DESPATCH	C.	Impressively great in size, force, or extent; enormous
T - 4. ACQUIESCED	D.	Formal, written requests for something needed
W - 5. RETICENT	E.	Reason with someone in an effort to dissuade or correct
A - 6. ASSIMILATION	F.	Charge for the carrying of burdens or goods as done by porters
U - 7. DISTILS	G.	Questioned; inquired
C - 8. PRODIGIOUS	H.	Struck down or hit
K - 9. AGUE	I.	Reduced in amount, degree, or intensity
I - 10. ABATED	J.	Written, official message sent with speed
X - 11. MALODOROUS	K.	Chill or fit of shivering
M - 12. AFFLICT	L.	With care and persistence
F - 13. PORTERAGE	M.	Inflict grievous physical or mental suffering on
Q - 14. VERBATIM	N.	Polite, refined, and often elegant in manner
N - 15. URBANE	O.	Causing annoyance, weariness, or vexation
P - 16. ALACRITY	P.	Cheerful willingness; eagerness; speed or quickness
O - 17. IRKSOME	Q.	In exactly the same words; word for word
E - 18. EXPOSTULATE	R.	Scene in which figures are arranged in a naturalistic setting against a painted background
Y - 19. SUCCUMBED	S.	Heavy, uncontrolled outpouring
V - 20. IMPREGNABLE	T.	Consented or complied passively or without protest
G - 21. QUERIED	U.	Separates or purifies
D - 22. REQUISITIONS	V.	Impossible to capture or enter by force
S - 23. TORRENT	W.	Inclined to keep one's thoughts, feelings, and personal affairs to oneself
H - 24. SMOTE	X.	Having a bad odor; foul
R - 25. DIORAMA	Y.	Yielded to an overwhelming desire; gave up or gave in

Dracula Vocabulary Matching 3

___ 1. LAIR
___ 2. INQUISITION
___ 3. SUCCUMBED
___ 4. CHAGRIN
___ 5. EMINENCE
___ 6. IMPREGNABLE
___ 7. INQUIETUDE
___ 8. SATURNINE
___ 9. CONSTRAINED
___ 10. PLACIDITY
___ 11. PALLOR
___ 12. ALACRITY
___ 13. ENIGMATICAL
___ 14. CONSIGNING
___ 15. THWARTING
___ 16. IMPERTURBABLE
___ 17. PRESAGE
___ 18. POIGNANT
___ 19. MALADY
___ 20. ABASEMENT
___ 21. AMENABLE
___ 22. ASSIMILATION
___ 23. RESUMPTION
___ 24. SANGUINE
___ 25. UNHALLOWED

A. Position of great distinction or superiority
B. Den or dwelling of a wild animal; a hideaway
C. Cheerful willingness; eagerness; speed or quickness
D. State of restlessness or uneasiness
E. Distressing to the mind or feelings; profoundly moving or touching
F. Strong feelings of embarrassment
G. Opposing and defeating the efforts, plans, or ambitions of something
H. Quality of being undisturbed by tumult or disorder; relaxation
I. Responsive to advice, authority, or suggestion; willing
J. Low or downcast state
K. Giving over to the care of another
L. Cheerfully confident; optimistic; of a healthy reddish color
M. In a forced or inhibited manner
N. The act of inquiring into a matter; an investigation
O. Impossible to capture or enter by force
P. Unholy
Q. Unshakably calm and collected
R. Disease, disorder, or ailment
S. Beginning again
T. Adopting the customs and attitudes of the prevailing culture
U. Yielded to an overwhelming desire; gave up or gave in
V. Extreme or unnatural paleness
W. Puzzling or mysterious
X. Melancholy or sullen; tending to be bitter
Y. Indication or warning of a future occurrence; an omen

Dracula Vocabulary Matching 3 Answer Key

B - 1.	LAIR	A. Position of great distinction or superiority
N - 2.	INQUISITION	B. Den or dwelling of a wild animal; a hideaway
U - 3.	SUCCUMBED	C. Cheerful willingness; eagerness; speed or quickness
F - 4.	CHAGRIN	D. State of restlessness or uneasiness
A - 5.	EMINENCE	E. Distressing to the mind or feelings; profoundly moving or touching
O - 6.	IMPREGNABLE	F. Strong feelings of embarrassment
D - 7.	INQUIETUDE	G. Opposing and defeating the efforts, plans, or ambitions of something
X - 8.	SATURNINE	H. Quality of being undisturbed by tumult or disorder; relaxation
M - 9.	CONSTRAINED	I. Responsive to advice, authority, or suggestion; willing
H - 10.	PLACIDITY	J. Low or downcast state
V - 11.	PALLOR	K. Giving over to the care of another
C - 12.	ALACRITY	L. Cheerfully confident; optimistic; of a healthy reddish color
W - 13.	ENIGMATICAL	M. In a forced or inhibited manner
K - 14.	CONSIGNING	N. The act of inquiring into a matter; an investigation
G - 15.	THWARTING	O. Impossible to capture or enter by force
Q - 16.	IMPERTURBABLE	P. Unholy
Y - 17.	PRESAGE	Q. Unshakably calm and collected
E - 18.	POIGNANT	R. Disease, disorder, or ailment
R - 19.	MALADY	S. Beginning again
J - 20.	ABASEMENT	T. Adopting the customs and attitudes of the prevailing culture
I - 21.	AMENABLE	U. Yielded to an overwhelming desire; gave up or gave in
T - 22.	ASSIMILATION	V. Extreme or unnatural paleness
S - 23.	RESUMPTION	W. Puzzling or mysterious
L - 24.	SANGUINE	X. Melancholy or sullen; tending to be bitter
P - 25.	UNHALLOWED	Y. Indication or warning of a future occurrence; an omen

Dracula Vocabulary Matching 4

___ 1. SATURNINE   A. Not spoken
___ 2. TETHER   B. In a state of profound awe and respect and often love
___ 3. PRESAGE   C. Intense ill will or hatred; great malice
___ 4. MALIGNITY   D. Beginning again
___ 5. RESUMPTION   E. Low or downcast state
___ 6. PALLOR   F. Melancholy or sullen; tending to be bitter
___ 7. VERBATIM   G. Sudden outburst of emotion or action
___ 8. POIGNANT   H. The act of inquiring into a matter; an investigation
___ 9. REVERENTLY   I. Deliberate triggering of trouble or discord
___10. TUMULT   J. In a forced or inhibited manner
___11. THWARTING   K. Drove away; dispersed
___12. MENIAL   L. Questioned; inquired
___13. UNFETTERED   M. Extreme or unnatural paleness
___14. CONVERGED   N. Restrain for holding an animal in place
___15. INSTIGATION   O. Confused or jumbled mass
___16. CONSTRAINED   P. Agitation of the mind or emotions
___17. QUERIED   Q. Set free or kept free from restrictions or bonds
___18. INQUISITION   R. Indication or warning of a future occurrence; an omen
___19. DISSIPATED   S. Distressing to the mind or feelings; profoundly moving or touching
___20. ADDUCE   T. Opposing and defeating the efforts, plans, or ambitions of something
___21. RETICENT   U. Relating to work regarded as for a servant
___22. TACIT   V. In exactly the same words; word for word
___23. ABASEMENT   W. Inclined to keep one's thoughts, feelings, and personal affairs to oneself
___24. AGGLOMERATION   X. Cite as an example or means of proof in an argument
___25. PAROXYSM   Y. Came together from different directions

Dracula Vocabulary Matching 4 Answer Key

F - 1.	SATURNINE	A. Not spoken
N - 2.	TETHER	B. In a state of profound awe and respect and often love
R - 3.	PRESAGE	C. Intense ill will or hatred; great malice
C - 4.	MALIGNITY	D. Beginning again
D - 5.	RESUMPTION	E. Low or downcast state
M - 6.	PALLOR	F. Melancholy or sullen; tending to be bitter
V - 7.	VERBATIM	G. Sudden outburst of emotion or action
S - 8.	POIGNANT	H. The act of inquiring into a matter; an investigation
B - 9.	REVERENTLY	I. Deliberate triggering of trouble or discord
P - 10.	TUMULT	J. In a forced or inhibited manner
T - 11.	THWARTING	K. Drove away; dispersed
U - 12.	MENIAL	L. Questioned; inquired
Q - 13.	UNFETTERED	M. Extreme or unnatural paleness
Y - 14.	CONVERGED	N. Restrain for holding an animal in place
I - 15.	INSTIGATION	O. Confused or jumbled mass
J - 16.	CONSTRAINED	P. Agitation of the mind or emotions
L - 17.	QUERIED	Q. Set free or kept free from restrictions or bonds
H - 18.	INQUISITION	R. Indication or warning of a future occurrence; an omen
K - 19.	DISSIPATED	S. Distressing to the mind or feelings; profoundly moving or touching
X - 20.	ADDUCE	T. Opposing and defeating the efforts, plans, or ambitions of something
W - 21.	RETICENT	U. Relating to work regarded as for a servant
A - 22.	TACIT	V. In exactly the same words; word for word
E - 23.	ABASEMENT	W. Inclined to keep one's thoughts, feelings, and personal affairs to oneself
O - 24.	AGGLOMERATION	X. Cite as an example or means of proof in an argument
G - 25.	PAROXYSM	Y. Came together from different directions

Dracula Vocabulary Magic Squares 1

Match the definition with the vocabulary word. Put your answers in the magic squares below. When your answers are correct, all columns and rows will add to the same number.

A. DEFERENCE
B. INQUIETUDE
C. PROLIFIC
D. MALIGNITY
E. CONSIGNING
F. ENIGMATICAL
G. DISPOSITION
H. INTRIGUED
I. ASSIDUOUSLY
J. MAELSTROM
K. HAGGARD
L. DIORAMA
M. EMACIATED
N. ADDENDUM
O. PROSAIC
P. DEMURRED

1. State of restlessness or uneasiness
2. One's usual mood; temperament
3. Appearing worn and exhausted
4. Something added or to be added, as in a supplement to a book
5. Extremely thin, especially as a result of starvation
6. Scene in which figures are arranged in a naturalistic setting against a painted background
7. Engaged in secret or underhanded schemes; spied
8. Yielding to the opinion, wishes, or judgment of another
9. Voiced opposition; objected
10. With care and persistence
11. Giving over to the care of another
12. Intense ill will or hatred; great malice
13. Producing abundant works or results
14. Puzzling or mysterious
15. Violent or turbulent situation; a large, violent whirlpool
16. Matter-of-fact; straightforward; lacking imagination; dull

A=	B=	C=	D=
E=	F=	G=	H=
I=	J=	K=	L=
M=	N=	O=	P=

Dracula Vocabulary Magic Squares 1 Answer Key

Match the definition with the vocabulary word. Put your answers in the magic squares below. When your answers are correct, all columns and rows will add to the same number.

A. DEFERENCE
B. INQUIETUDE
C. PROLIFIC
D. MALIGNITY
E. CONSIGNING
F. ENIGMATICAL
G. DISPOSITION
H. INTRIGUED
I. ASSIDUOUSLY
J. MAELSTROM
K. HAGGARD
L. DIORAMA
M. EMACIATED
N. ADDENDUM
O. PROSAIC
P. DEMURRED

1. State of restlessness or uneasiness
2. One's usual mood; temperament
3. Appearing worn and exhausted
4. Something added or to be added, as in a supplement to a book
5. Extremely thin, especially as a result of starvation
6. Scene in which figures are arranged in a naturalistic setting against a painted background
7. Engaged in secret or underhanded schemes; spied
8. Yielding to the opinion, wishes, or judgment of another
9. Voiced opposition; objected
10. With care and persistence
11. Giving over to the care of another
12. Intense ill will or hatred; great malice
13. Producing abundant works or results
14. Puzzling or mysterious
15. Violent or turbulent situation; a large, violent whirlpool
16. Matter-of-fact; straightforward; lacking imagination; dull

A=8	B=1	C=13	D=12
E=11	F=14	G=2	H=7
I=10	J=15	K=3	L=6
M=5	N=4	O=16	P=9

Dracula Vocabulary Magic Squares 2

Match the definition with the vocabulary word. Put your answers in the magic squares below. When your answers are correct, all columns and rows will add to the same number.

A. ABATED
B. REQUISITIONS
C. BOUDOIR
D. PORTERAGE
E. IRKSOME
F. PRESAGE
G. WILY
H. ASSIMILATION
I. IMPERTURBABLE
J. TRENCHANT
K. ALACRITY
L. VIADUCT
M. DISSIPATED
N. ASSAIL
O. PALLOR
P. POIGNANT

1. Attack, as with ridicule
2. Marked by skill in deception
3. Bridge consisting of arches used to carry a road over a valley
4. Reduced in amount, degree, or intensity
5. Cheerful willingness; eagerness; speed or quickness
6. Formal, written requests for something needed
7. Drove away; dispersed
8. Adopting the customs and attitudes of the prevailing culture
9. Causing annoyance, weariness, or vexation
10. Distressing to the mind or feelings; profoundly moving or touching
11. Woman's private sitting room, dressing room, or bedroom
12. Forceful, effective, and vigorous
13. Charge for the carrying of burdens or goods as done by porters
14. Unshakably calm and collected
15. Indication or warning of a future occurrence; an omen
16. Extreme or unnatural paleness

A=	B=	C=	D=
E=	F=	G=	H=
I=	J=	K=	L=
M=	N=	O=	P=

Dracula Vocabulary Magic Squares 2 Answer Key

Match the definition with the vocabulary word. Put your answers in the magic squares below. When your answers are correct, all columns and rows will add to the same number.

A. ABATED
B. REQUISITIONS
C. BOUDOIR
D. PORTERAGE
E. IRKSOME
F. PRESAGE
G. WILY
H. ASSIMILATION
I. IMPERTURBABLE
J. TRENCHANT
K. ALACRITY
L. VIADUCT
M. DISSIPATED
N. ASSAIL
O. PALLOR
P. POIGNANT

1. Attack, as with ridicule
2. Marked by skill in deception
3. Bridge consisting of arches used to carry a road over a valley
4. Reduced in amount, degree, or intensity
5. Cheerful willingness; eagerness; speed or quickness
6. Formal, written requests for something needed
7. Drove away; dispersed
8. Adopting the customs and attitudes of the prevailing culture
9. Causing annoyance, weariness, or vexation
10. Distressing to the mind or feelings; profoundly moving or touching
11. Woman's private sitting room, dressing room, or bedroom
12. Forceful, effective, and vigorous
13. Charge for the carrying of burdens or goods as done by porters
14. Unshakably calm and collected
15. Indication or warning of a future occurrence; an omen
16. Extreme or unnatural paleness

A=4	B=6	C=11	D=13
E=9	F=15	G=2	H=8
I=14	J=12	K=5	L=3
M=7	N=1	O=16	P=10

Dracula Vocabulary Magic Squares 3

Match the definition with the vocabulary word. Put your answers in the magic squares below. When your answers are correct, all columns and rows will add to the same number.

A. INTRIGUED
B. MAELSTROM
C. INSTIGATION
D. IMPLICITLY
E. AFFLICT
F. DESPATCH
G. VERBATIM
H. PRODIGIOUS
I. REQUISITIONS
J. RETICENT
K. ENIGMATICAL
L. AVARICE
M. DEBAUCH
N. IMPERTURBABLE
O. PLACIDITY
P. SUCCUMBED

1. Impressively great in size, force, or extent; enormous
2. Corrupt morally
3. Violent or turbulent situation; a large, violent whirlpool
4. Puzzling or mysterious
5. Inclined to keep one's thoughts, feelings, and personal affairs to oneself
6. Deliberate triggering of trouble or discord
7. Yielded to an overwhelming desire; gave up or gave in
8. Inflict grievous physical or mental suffering on
9. Quality of being undisturbed by tumult or disorder; relaxation
10. Written, official message sent with speed
11. Formal, written requests for something needed
12. In a manner which is understood though not directly expressed
13. Engaged in secret or underhanded schemes; spied
14. Immoderate desire for wealth; greed
15. In exactly the same words; word for word
16. Unshakably calm and collected

A=	B=	C=	D=
E=	F=	G=	H=
I=	J=	K=	L=
M=	N=	O=	P=

Dracula Vocabulary Magic Squares 3 Answer Key

Match the definition with the vocabulary word. Put your answers in the magic squares below. When your answers are correct, all columns and rows will add to the same number.

A. INTRIGUED
B. MAELSTROM
C. INSTIGATION
D. IMPLICITLY
E. AFFLICT
F. DESPATCH
G. VERBATIM
H. PRODIGIOUS
I. REQUISITIONS
J. RETICENT
K. ENIGMATICAL
L. AVARICE
M. DEBAUCH
N. IMPERTURBABLE
O. PLACIDITY
P. SUCCUMBED

1. Impressively great in size, force, or extent; enormous
2. Corrupt morally
3. Violent or turbulent situation; a large, violent whirlpool
4. Puzzling or mysterious
5. Inclined to keep one's thoughts, feelings, and personal affairs to oneself
6. Deliberate triggering of trouble or discord
7. Yielded to an overwhelming desire; gave up or gave in
8. Inflict grievous physical or mental suffering on
9. Quality of being undisturbed by tumult or disorder; relaxation
10. Written, official message sent with speed
11. Formal, written requests for something needed
12. In a manner which is understood though not directly expressed
13. Engaged in secret or underhanded schemes; spied
14. Immoderate desire for wealth; greed
15. In exactly the same words; word for word
16. Unshakably calm and collected

A=13	B=3	C=6	D=12
E=8	F=10	G=15	H=1
I=11	J=5	K=4	L=14
M=2	N=16	O=9	P=7

Dracula Vocabulary Magic Squares 4

Match the definition with the vocabulary word. Put your answers in the magic squares below. When your answers are correct, all columns and rows will add to the same number.

A. CHAGRIN
B. ENIGMATICAL
C. ACCENTUATED
D. ELUDE
E. ASCERTAIN
F. REVERENTLY
G. BOUDOIR
H. REMONSTRANCE
I. VERBATIM
J. ODIUM
K. ACQUIESCED
L. IMPREGNABLE
M. MALADY
N. UNHALLOWED
O. PRODIGIOUS
P. ABATED

1. In a state of profound awe and respect and often love
2. In exactly the same words; word for word
3. Impressively great in size, force, or extent; enormous
4. Evade or escape from, as by daring, cleverness, or skill
5. Disease, disorder, or ailment
6. Puzzling or mysterious
7. Expression of protest or complaint
8. Consented or complied passively or without protest
9. Stressed or emphasized; intensified
10. Reduced in amount, degree, or intensity
11. Strong dislike, contempt or aversion
12. Make certain, definite, and precise
13. Impossible to capture or enter by force
14. Woman's private sitting room, dressing room, or bedroom
15. Strong feelings of embarrassment
16. Unholy

A=	B=	C=	D=
E=	F=	G=	H=
I=	J=	K=	L=
M=	N=	O=	P=

Dracula Vocabulary Magic Squares 4 Answer Key

Match the definition with the vocabulary word. Put your answers in the magic squares below. When your answers are correct, all columns and rows will add to the same number.

A. CHAGRIN
B. ENIGMATICAL
C. ACCENTUATED
D. ELUDE
E. ASCERTAIN
F. REVERENTLY
G. BOUDOIR
H. REMONSTRANCE
I. VERBATIM
J. ODIUM
K. ACQUIESCED
L. IMPREGNABLE
M. MALADY
N. UNHALLOWED
O. PRODIGIOUS
P. ABATED

1. In a state of profound awe and respect and often love
2. In exactly the same words; word for word
3. Impressively great in size, force, or extent; enormous
4. Evade or escape from, as by daring, cleverness, or skill
5. Disease, disorder, or ailment
6. Puzzling or mysterious
7. Expression of protest or complaint
8. Consented or complied passively or without protest
9. Stressed or emphasized; intensified
10. Reduced in amount, degree, or intensity
11. Strong dislike, contempt or aversion
12. Make certain, definite, and precise
13. Impossible to capture or enter by force
14. Woman's private sitting room, dressing room, or bedroom
15. Strong feelings of embarrassment
16. Unholy

A=15	B=6	C=9	D=4
E=12	F=1	G=14	H=7
I=2	J=11	K=8	L=13
M=5	N=16	O=3	P=10

Dracula Vocabulary Word Search 1

```
M D E F E R E N C E P A R O X Y S M
A I C A L M O E H H S F F G M V H G
L M D N C T D G A C C T K F F Z X K
A P R N X U P A G E N T A I L E D M
D L E E L Q M S R L V H M L S I M R
Y I S E T U C E I A D P A Z W H C A
V C O H E E O R N C E B R G J A S T
P I N K T R N P X R K O G G S R G
T T A L H I V S T D J U I N A A Q T
Z L N D E E E U J M M D I G X R H
V Y T E R D R W M A U O L N L V E D
F E Z T A B G C L M N I F G K M S P
M F R A A D E O S Z D R F I O K W T
H U S B A N D R Y M A E L S T R O M
T D L A A O Y U E G N K K N M R K N
A E A L R T L N C K E R Q O C O D V
C P G O I B I M Z E I Z L C M S T G
I Y U Q A A W M T O R R E N T Q K E
T S E S L I T S I D O D I U M V R H
```

Appearing worn and exhausted (7)
Attack, as with ridicule (6)
Came together from different directions (9)
Causing annoyance, weariness, or vexation (7)
Chill or fit of shivering (4)
Cite as an example or means of proof in an argument (6)
Den or dwelling of a wild animal; a hideaway (4)
Disease, disorder, or ailment (6)
Employee responsible for the upkeep of church property (6)
Evade or escape from, as by daring, cleverness, or skill (5)
Giving over to the care of another (10)
Having a bad odor; foul (10)
Having or marked by imposing physical strength (8)
Heavy, uncontrolled outpouring (7)
In a manner which is understood though not directly expressed (10)
In exactly the same words; word for word (8)
Indication or warning of a future occurrence; an omen (7)
Inflict grievous physical or mental suffering on (7)
Light carriage with two or four low wheels and a collapsible top (7)
Limited inheritance of property to specified heirs (8)
Marked by skill in deception (4)

Not spoken (5)
Practice of growing crops, & breeding and raising livestock (9)
Questioned; inquired (7)
Quickness, accuracy, and keenness of judgment or insight (6)
Reduced in amount, degree, or intensity (6)
Relating to commonplace things; ordinary (7)
Relating to work regarded as for a servant (6)
Restrain for holding an animal in place (6)
Scene in which figures are arranged in a naturalistic setting against a painted background (7)
Separates or purifies (7)
Strong and deep in tone (8)
Strong dislike, contempt or aversion (5)
Strong feelings of embarrassment (7)
Struck down or hit (5)
Sudden outburst of emotion or action (8)
Unshakably calm and collected (13)
Violent or turbulent situation; a large, violent whirlpool (9)
Woman's private sitting room, dressing room, or bedroom (7)
Yielding to the opinion, wishes, or judgment of another (9)

Dracula Vocabulary Word Search 1 Answer Key

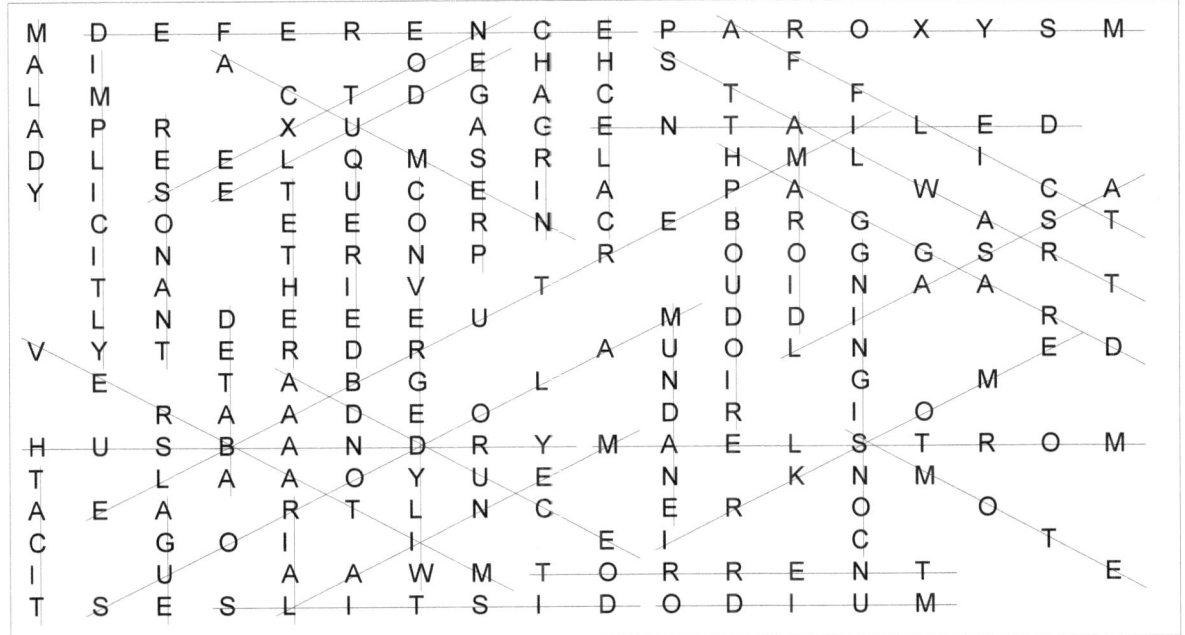

Appearing worn and exhausted (7)
Attack, as with ridicule (6)
Came together from different directions (9)
Causing annoyance, weariness, or vexation (7)
Chill or fit of shivering (4)
Cite as an example or means of proof in an argument (6)
Den or dwelling of a wild animal; a hideaway (4)
Disease, disorder, or ailment (6)
Employee responsible for the upkeep of church property (6)
Evade or escape from, as by daring, cleverness, or skill (5)
Giving over to the care of another (10)
Having a bad odor; foul (10)
Having or marked by imposing physical strength (8)
Heavy, uncontrolled outpouring (7)
In a manner which is understood though not directly expressed (10)
In exactly the same words; word for word (8)
Indication or warning of a future occurrence; an omen (7)
Inflict grievous physical or mental suffering on (7)
Light carriage with two or four low wheels and a collapsible top (7)
Limited inheritance of property to specified heirs (8)
Marked by skill in deception (4)
Not spoken (5)
Practice of growing crops, & breeding and raising livestock (9)
Questioned; inquired (7)
Quickness, accuracy, and keenness of judgment or insight (6)
Reduced in amount, degree, or intensity (6)
Relating to commonplace things; ordinary (7)
Relating to work regarded as for a servant (6)
Restrain for holding an animal in place (6)
Scene in which figures are arranged in a naturalistic setting against a painted background (7)
Separates or purifies (7)
Strong and deep in tone (8)
Strong dislike, contempt or aversion (5)
Strong feelings of embarrassment (7)
Struck down or hit (5)
Sudden outburst of emotion or action (8)
Unshakably calm and collected (13)
Violent or turbulent situation; a large, violent whirlpool (9)
Woman's private sitting room, dressing room, or bedroom (7)
Yielding to the opinion, wishes, or judgment of another (9)

Dracula Vocabulary Word Search 2

```
R E V E R E N T L Y A B A T E D H C
A C U M E N D I V I A D U C T S A J
U R B A N E A L A I N E M G F P G K
W I L Y I S T N M K R A R T R L G P
B E P R S L A C U G L P E O P A A X
G L E A I E A D I A R T S Y Z I R H
S U C C U M B E D E B A U C H R D G
Q D N R A A P Y O U I P M M G O W K
M E R R V C A O G C C W P I U L Y L
T W O S A I F A T C F E T N S L L J
P I Q E R A F M M E T T I Q M A T K
D A Q X I T L E H I N E O U O P I M
A Y R T C E I N C L E T N I T I C Z
G J N O E D C A T A C H I S E R I N
U L K N X V T B A N I E R I L K L Q
E P Y G M Y W L P G T R G T V S P C
D I S T I L S E S U E J A I W O M Y
F I S S U R E M E I R R H O T M I Q
V E R B A T I M D D R J C N H E P S
```

Agitation of the mind or emotions (6)
Appearing worn and exhausted (7)
Attack, as with ridicule (6)
Beginning again (10)
Bridge consisting of arches used to carry a road over a valley (7)
Causing annoyance, weariness, or vexation (7)
Chill or fit of shivering (4)
Cite as an example or means of proof in an argument (6)
Corrupt morally (7)
Den or dwelling of a wild animal; a hideaway (4)
Disease, disorder, or ailment (6)
Employee responsible for the upkeep of church property (6)
Evade or escape from, as by daring, cleverness, or skill (5)
Extreme or unnatural paleness (6)
Extremely thin, especially as a result of starvation (9)
Immoderate desire for wealth; greed (7)
In a manner which is understood though not directly expressed (10)
In a state of profound awe and respect and often love (10)
In exactly the same words; word for word (8)
Inclined to keep one's thoughts, feelings, and personal affairs to oneself (8)
Inflict grievous physical or mental suffering on (7)
Lacking energy or vitality; weak (7)
Lacking physical strength or vigor; weak (8)
Long, narrow opening; a crack or cleft (7)
Marked by skill in deception (4)
Matter-of-fact; straightforward; lacking imagination; dull (7)
Not spoken (5)
Polite, refined, and often elegant in manner (6)
Questioned; inquired (7)
Quickness, accuracy, and keenness of judgment or insight (6)
Reduced in amount, degree, or intensity (6)
Relating to work regarded as for a servant (6)
Responsive to advice, authority, or suggestion; willing (8)
Restrain for holding an animal in place (6)
Scene in which figures are arranged in a naturalistic setting against a painted background (7)
Separates or purifies (7)
Strong dislike, contempt or aversion (5)
Strong feelings of embarrassment (7)
Struck down or hit (5)
Sudden outburst of emotion or action (8)
The act of inquiring into a matter; an investigation (11)
Written, official message sent with speed (8)
Yielded to an overwhelming desire; gave up or gave in (9)

Dracula Vocabulary Word Search 2 Answer Key

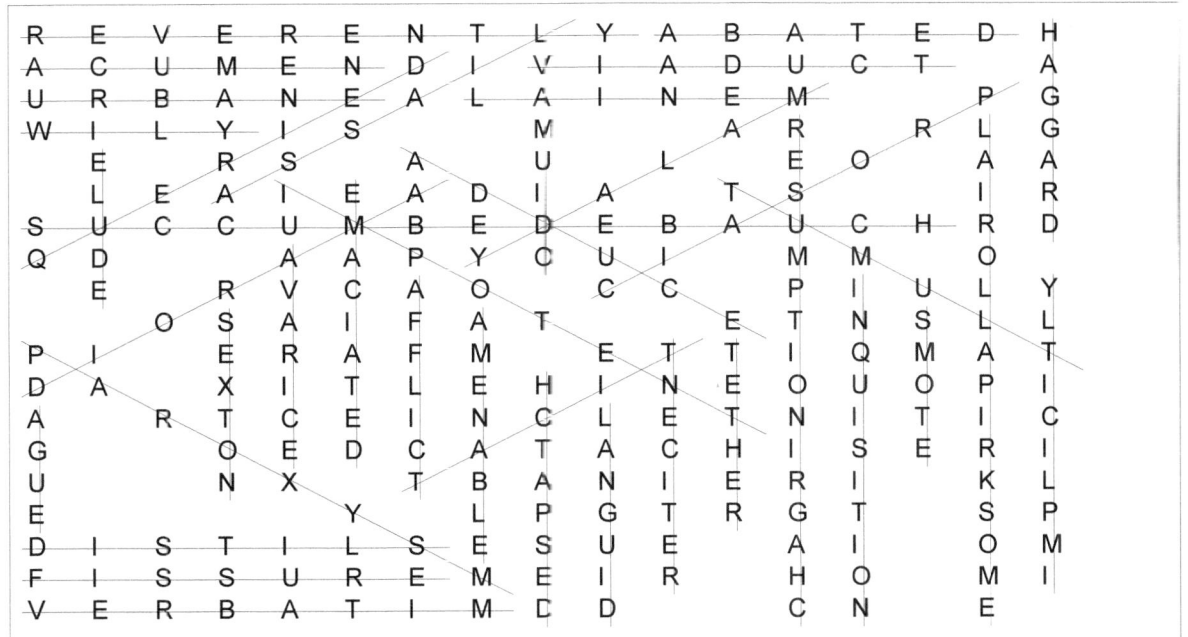

Agitation of the mind or emotions (6)
Appearing worn and exhausted (7)
Attack, as with ridicule (6)
Beginning again (10)
Bridge consisting of arches used to carry a road over a valley (7)
Causing annoyance, weariness, or vexation (7)
Chill or fit of shivering (4)
Cite as an example or means of proof in an argument (6)
Corrupt morally (7)
Den or dwelling of a wild animal; a hideaway (4)
Disease, disorder, or ailment (6)
Employee responsible for the upkeep of church property (6)
Evade or escape from, as by daring, cleverness, or skill (5)
Extreme or unnatural paleness (6)
Extremely thin, especially as a result of starvation (9)
Immoderate desire for wealth; greed (7)
In a manner which is understood though not directly expressed (10)
In a state of profound awe and respect and often love (10)
In exactly the same words; word for word (8)
Inclined to keep one's thoughts, feelings, and personal affairs to oneself (8)
Inflict grievous physical or mental suffering on (7)
Lacking energy or vitality; weak (7)
Lacking physical strength or vigor; weak (8)
Long, narrow opening; a crack or cleft (7)
Marked by skill in deception (4)
Matter-of-fact; straightforward; lacking imagination; dull (7)
Not spoken (5)
Polite, refined, and often elegant in manner (6)
Questioned; inquired (7)
Quickness, accuracy, and keenness of judgment or insight (6)
Reduced in amount, degree, or intensity (6)
Relating to work regarded as for a servant (6)
Responsive to advice, authority, or suggestion; willing (8)
Restrain for holding an animal in place (6)
Scene in which figures are arranged in a naturalistic setting against a painted background (7)
Separates or purifies (7)
Strong dislike, contempt or aversion (5)
Strong feelings of embarrassment (7)
Struck down or hit (5)
Sudden outburst of emotion or action (8)
The act of inquiring into a matter; an investigation (11)
Written, official message sent with speed (8)
Yielded to an overwhelming desire; gave up or gave in (9)

Dracula Vocabulary Word Search 3

```
R E V E R E N T L Y R D N A B S U H I S
E E K O A E N L U M E N I A L R N O M T
P F S R L B S I R M H S N Y B P N O P L
U R L U J U A O G H U Q W A J R F D E H
D E T O M S P S N M T L N C P O O W R X
I A W S I P B T E A A E T G O S T I T J
A S B E T M T N U M M N T M W I A N U S
T S H X A F P I M O E E T I U G I K R G
E A D T B T P R O M U N X C N C E T B S
D I Z O R S L G E N A S T D A D D R A R
M L W N E L Z A Z G C L Y P N L A E B V
A X X I V W D H E T N T A B T A S N L W
E H C E L A C C N K I A D D U C E C E B
L I W H G Y I E F D D N B N Y U H H T T
S M N K T R C T I D R E T L G M G A C T
T P Y Y A I R C E O R G Z R E E A N T T
R L R V T A A N L U H Y L D I N M T A L
O I A E W L D L S D P R E S A G E W P M
M C R L P U A S H E Q L P C S R U B S L
G I A Y M P I Y T T I Q P N I G L E E E
R T C I L F F A C A H S L A N G U I D G
S L I T S I D J T B C W L V O D I U M H
P Y T O R R E N T A S I C I F I L O R P
M H C O N V E R G E D G T L T E T H E R
```

ABASEMENT	CONVERGED	IMPREGNABLE	POIGNANT	STALWART
ABATED	DESPATCH	INTRIGUED	PRESAGE	TACIT
ACUMEN	DISTILS	LAIR	PROLIFIC	TETHER
ADDENDUM	ELUDE	LANGUID	PROSAIC	TORRENT
ADDUCE	ENIGMATICAL	MAELSTROM	REPUDIATED	TRENCHANT
AFFLICT	ENTAILED	MALADY	RESONANT	TUMULT
AGUE	FISSURE	MENIAL	RESUMPTION	UNFETTERED
ASSAIL	HOODWINK	MUNDANE	RETICENT	URBANE
AVARICE	HUSBANDRY	ODIUM	REVERENTLY	VERBATIM
CALECHE	IMPERTURBABLE	PALLOR	SEXTON	VOLUPTUOUS
CHAGRIN	IMPLICITLY	PLACIDITY	SMOTE	WILY

Dracula Vocabulary Word Search 3 Answer Key

ABASEMENT	CONVERGED	IMPREGNABLE	POIGNANT	STALWART
ABATED	DESPATCH	INTRIGUED	PRESAGE	TACIT
ACUMEN	DISTILS	LAIR	PROLIFIC	TETHER
ADDENDUM	ELUDE	LANGUID	PROSAIC	TORRENT
ADDUCE	ENIGMATICAL	MAELSTROM	REPUDIATED	TRENCHANT
AFFLICT	ENTAILED	MALADY	RESONANT	TUMULT
AGUE	FISSURE	MENIAL	RESUMPTION	UNFETTERED
ASSAIL	HOODWINK	MUNDANE	RETICENT	URBANE
AVARICE	HUSBANDRY	ODIUM	REVERENTLY	VERBATIM
CALECHE	IMPERTURBABLE	PALLOR	SEXTON	VOLUPTUOUS
CHAGRIN	IMPLICITLY	PLACIDITY	SMOTE	WILY

Dracula Vocabulary Word Search 4

```
T N E T O P M I H P P V E R B A T I M R
R H T D C L A R O V R I S A N G U I N E
E N W L Z N L K O M O O N A F F L I C T
N I A A L W A S D F S S L T Y K Q R F H
C A S S R T D O W G A T D I R Y L I W W
H T S M S T Y M I D I A O J F I J O Y N
A R K S O A I E N I C L D R U I G D H K
N E Q A I T I N K S E W N D R B C U L Y
T C N V K D E L G T L A E P B E K O E B
M S T A S P U A N I U R U L A D N B C D
R A S R R L Z O S L D T G J N V Z T R Y
E M Y I E B T P U S E G A S E R P M E M
Q E L C V X P A M S I N N I R G A H C E
U N T E E A R L U A L M A D D U C E C K
I A I S R C O L D Z L Y I D N E W N P B
S B C L E U D O N G C I I L L F E A J G
I L I W N M I R E Y B U G A A R L M R S
T E L L T E G N D G G G C N E T A A Y T
I U P Z L N I T D N Y T M F I B I R Q J
O M M S Y X O R A P M A E L S T R O M X
N N I U D T U L K C U D N T B V Y I N P
S W C C L R S V Q D I N I Y H P J D C D
U N F E T T E R E D D T A F D E T A B A
F I S S U R E L G F O P L Q U E R I E D
```

ABATED	AVARICE	IMPOTENT	PAROXYSM	STALWART
ACUMEN	BOUDOIR	INTRIGUED	PRESAGE	TACIT
ADDENDUM	CALECHE	IRKSOME	PRODIGIOUS	TETHER
ADDUCE	CHAGRIN	LAIR	PROLIFIC	THWARTING
AFFLICT	DEFERENCE	LANGUID	PROSAIC	TORRENT
AGUE	DIORAMA	MAELSTROM	QUERIED	TRENCHANT
AMENABLE	DISTILS	MALADY	REQUISITIONS	TUMULT
ASCERTAIN	ELUDE	MALIGNITY	REVERENTLY	UNFETTERED
ASSAIL	FISSURE	MENIAL	SANGUINE	URBANE
ASSIDUOUSLY	HOODWINK	ODIUM	SEXTON	VERBATIM
ASSIMILATION	IMPLICITLY	PALLOR	SMOTE	WILY

Dracula Vocabulary Word Search 4 Answer Key

ABATED	AVARICE	IMPOTENT	PAROXYSM	STALWART
ACUMEN	BOUDOIR	INTRIGUED	PRESAGE	TACIT
ADDENDUM	CALECHE	IRKSOME	PRODIGIOUS	TETHER
ADDUCE	CHAGRIN	LAIR	PROLIFIC	THWARTING
AFFLICT	DEFERENCE	LANGUID	PROSAIC	TORRENT
AGUE	DIORAMA	MAELSTROM	QUERIED	TRENCHANT
AMENABLE	DISTILS	MALADY	REQUISITIONS	TUMULT
ASCERTAIN	ELUDE	MALIGNITY	REVERENTLY	UNFETTERED
ASSAIL	FISSURE	MENIAL	SANGUINE	URBANE
ASSIDUOUSLY	HOODWINK	ODIUM	SEXTON	VERBATIM
ASSIMILATION	IMPLICITLY	PALLOR	SMOTE	WILY

Dracula Vocabulary Crossword 1

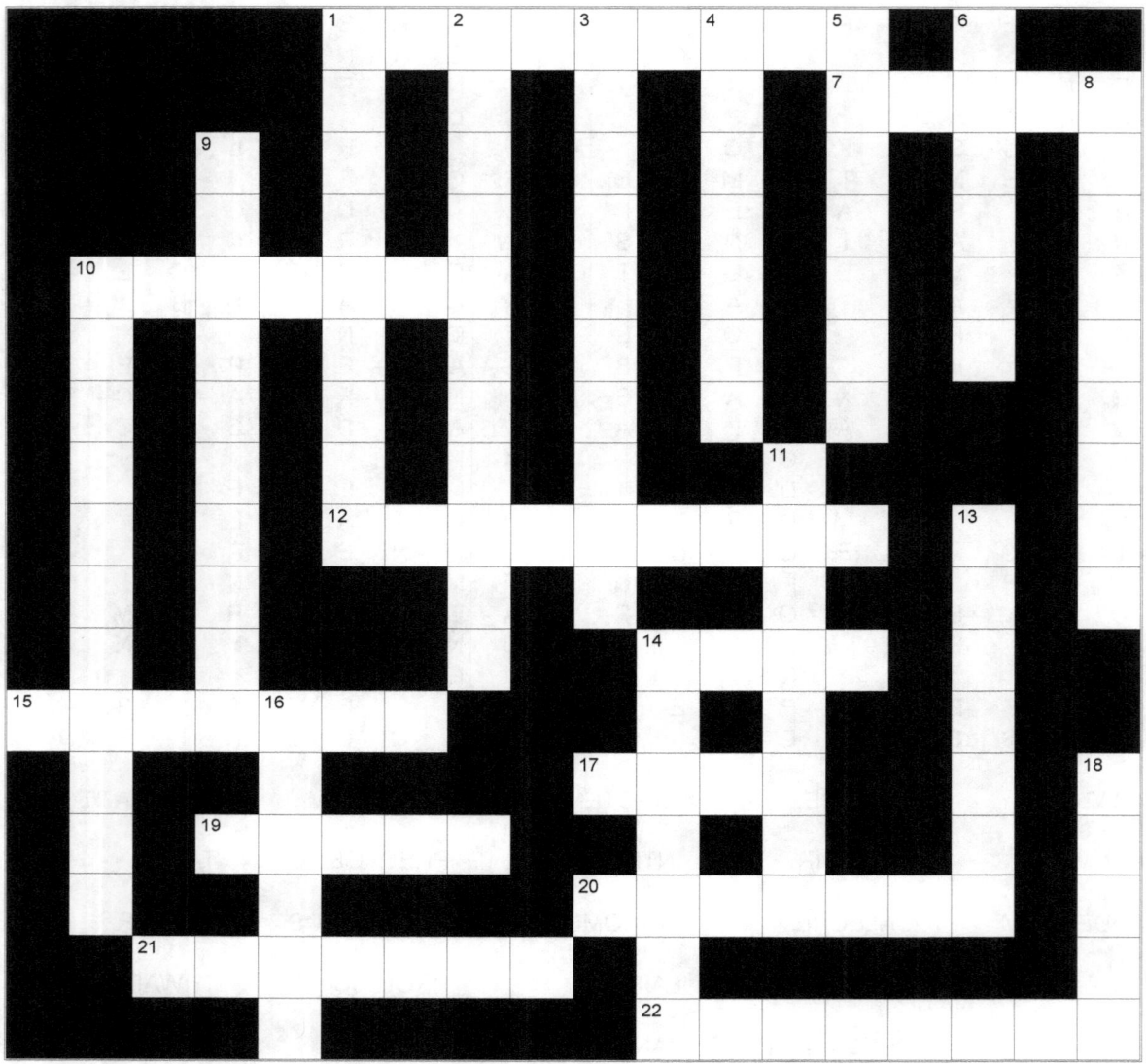

Across
1. Yielded to an overwhelming desire; gave up or gave in
7. Evade or escape from, as by daring, cleverness, or skill
10. Inflict grievous physical or mental suffering on
12. Came together from different directions
14. Chill or fit of shivering
15. Relating to commonplace things; ordinary
17. Den or dwelling of a wild animal; a hideaway
19. Not spoken
20. Bridge consisting of arches used to carry a road over a valley
21. Indication or warning of a future occurrence; an omen
22. Position of great distinction or superiority

Down
1. Characteristic of a scholar or thinker
2. In a forced or inhibited manner
3. Unholy
4. Woman's private sitting room, dressing room, or bedroom
5. Corrupt morally
6. Agitation of the mind or emotions
8. Extremely thin, especially as a result of starvation
9. Set free or kept free from restrictions or bonds
10. With care and persistence
11. Voiced opposition; objected
13. Heavy, uncontrolled outpouring
14. Immoderate desire for wealth; greed
16. Reduced in amount, degree, or intensity
18. Struck down or hit

Dracula Vocabulary Crossword 1 Answer Key

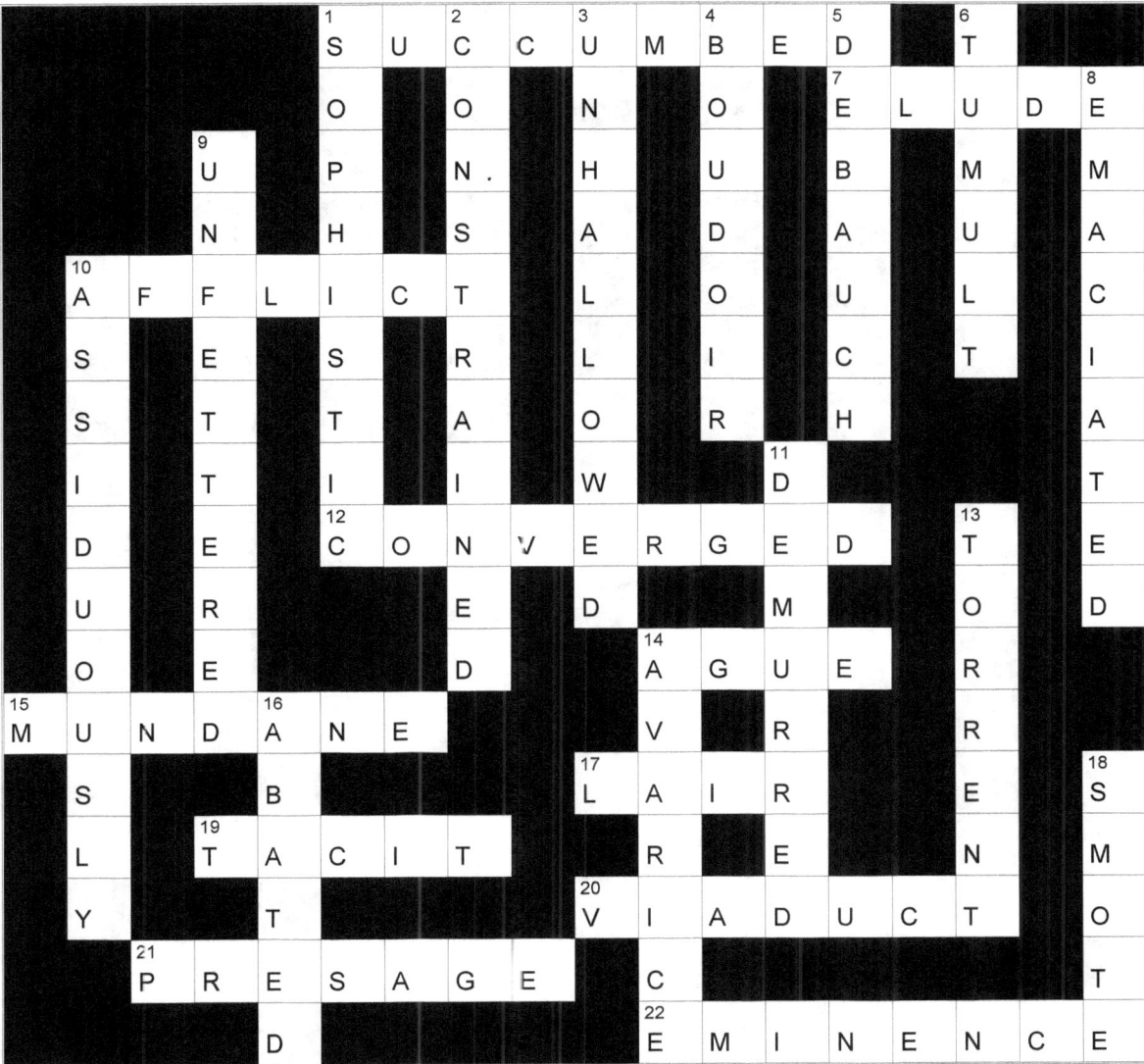

Across
1. Yielded to an overwhelming desire; gave up or gave in
7. Evade or escape from, as by daring, cleverness, or skill
10. Inflict grievous physical or mental suffering on
12. Came together from different directions
14. Chill or fit of shivering
15. Relating to commonplace things; ordinary
17. Den or dwelling of a wild animal; a hideaway
19. Not spoken
20. Bridge consisting of arches used to carry a road over a valley
21. Indication or warning of a future occurrence; an omen
22. Position of great distinction or superiority

Down
1. Characteristic of a scholar or thinker
2. In a forced or inhibited manner
3. Unholy
4. Woman's private sitting room, dressing room, or bedroom
5. Corrupt morally
6. Agitation of the mind or emotions
8. Extremely thin, especially as a result of starvation
9. Set free or kept free from restrictions or bonds
10. With care and persistence
11. Voiced opposition; objected
13. Heavy, uncontrolled outpouring
14. Immoderate desire for wealth; greed
16. Reduced in amount, degree, or intensity
18. Struck down or hit

Dracula Vocabulary Crossword 2

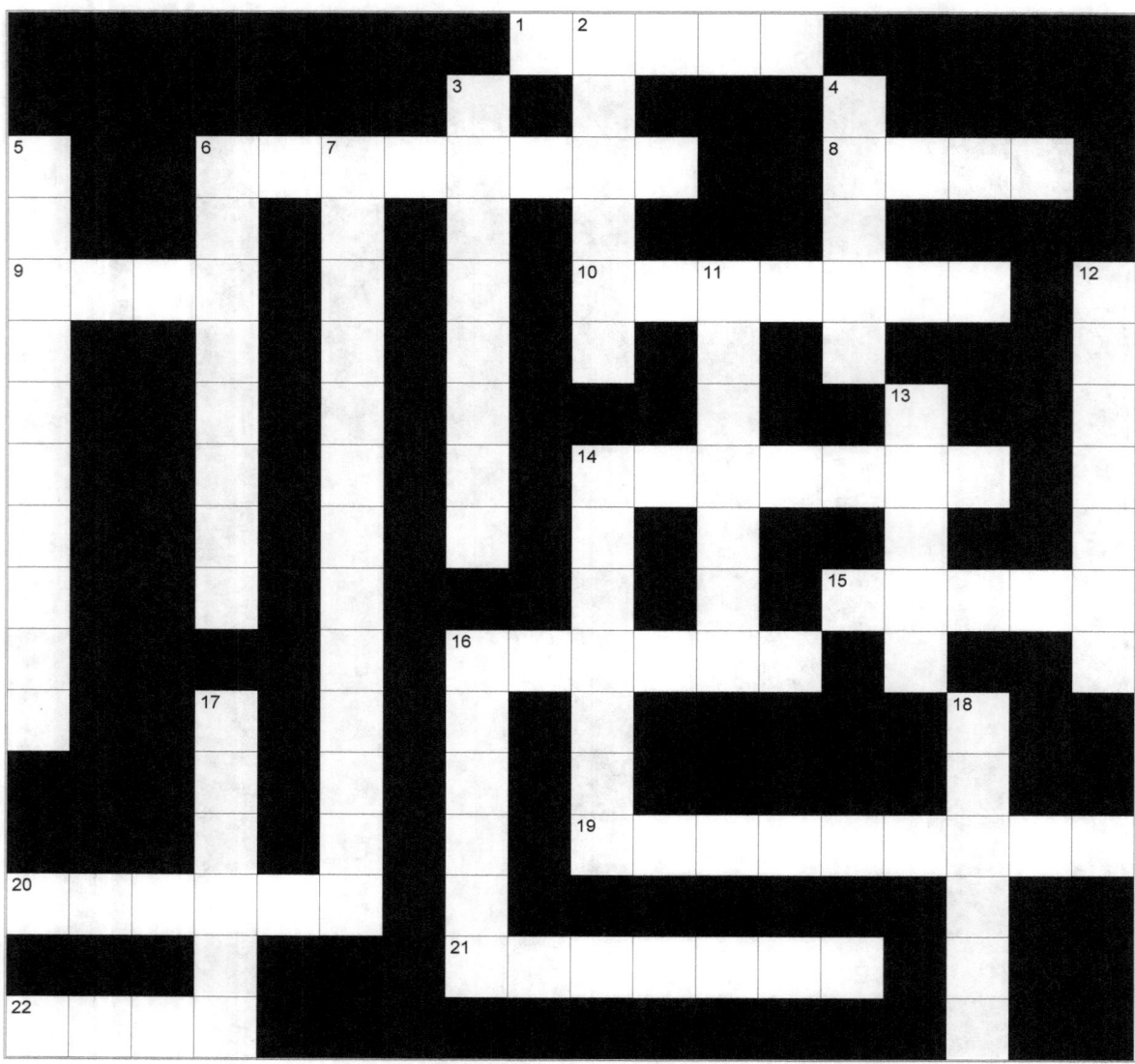

Across
1. Struck down or hit
6. Distressing to the mind or feelings; profoundly moving or touching
8. Chill or fit of shivering
9. Den or dwelling of a wild animal; a hideaway
10. Inflict grievous physical or mental suffering on
14. Separates or purifies
15. Strong dislike, contempt or aversion
16. Reduced in amount, degree, or intensity
19. Practice of growing crops, & breeding and raising livestock
20. Polite, refined, and often elegant in manner
21. Lacking energy or vitality; weak
22. Marked by skill in deception

Down
2. Relating to work regarded as for a servant
3. Limited inheritance of property to specified heirs
4. Not spoken
5. Arising from or contributing to the satisfaction of sensual desires
6. Sudden outburst of emotion or action
7. Unshakably calm and collected
11. Long, narrow opening; a crack or cleft
12. Causing annoyance, weariness, or vexation
13. Evade or escape from, as by daring, cleverness, or skill
14. Corrupt morally
16. Attack, as with ridicule
17. Disease, disorder, or ailment
18. Cite as an example or means of proof in an argument

Dracula Vocabulary Crossword 2 Answer Key

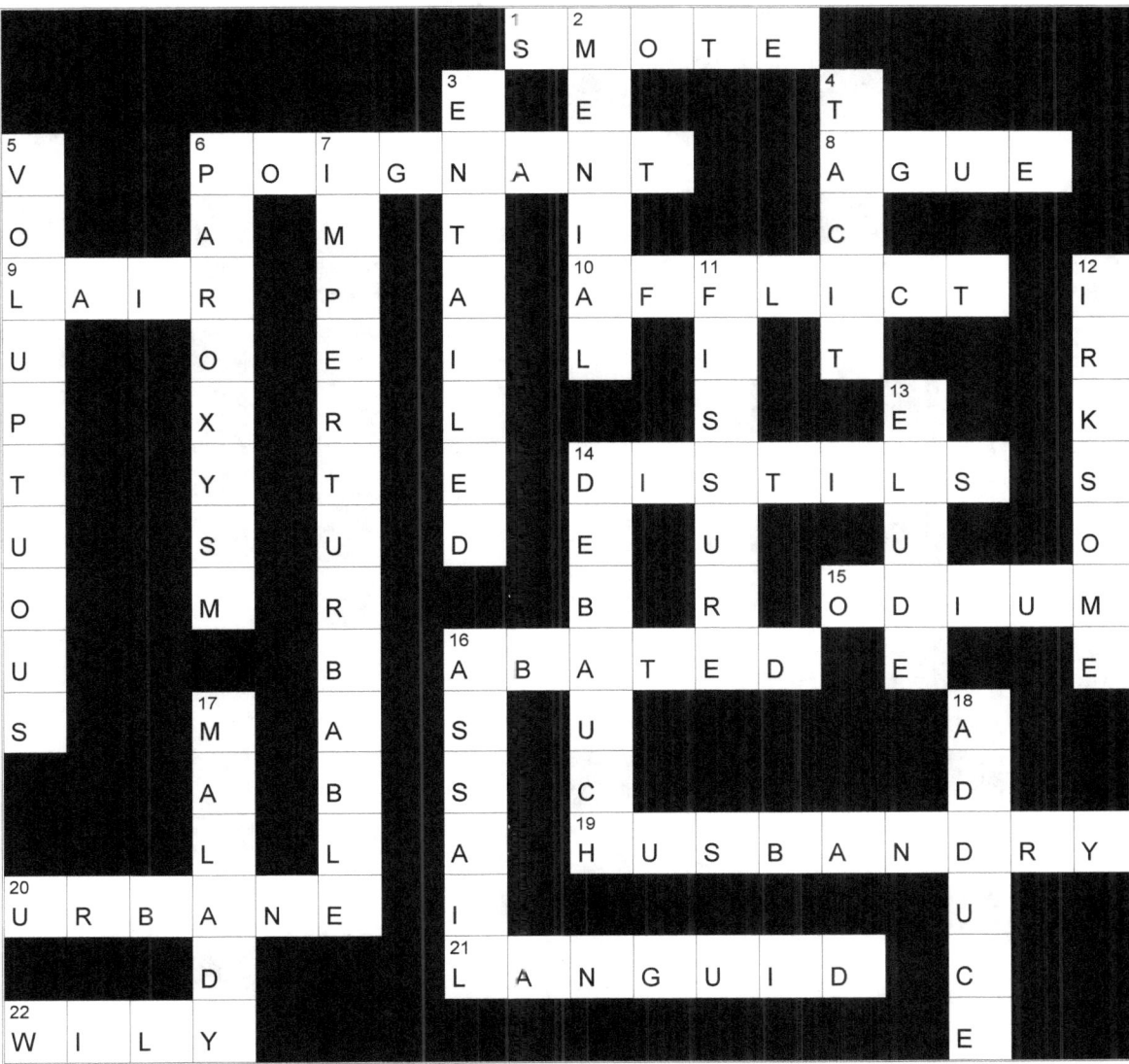

Across
1. Struck down or hit
6. Distressing to the mind or feelings; profoundly moving or touching
8. Chill or fit of shivering
9. Den or dwelling of a wild animal; a hideaway
10. Inflict grievous physical or mental suffering on
14. Separates or purifies
15. Strong dislike, contempt or aversion
16. Reduced in amount, degree, or intensity
19. Practice of growing crops, & breeding and raising livestock
20. Polite, refined, and often elegant in manner
21. Lacking energy or vitality; weak
22. Marked by skill in deception

Down
2. Relating to work regarded as for a servant
3. Limited inheritance of property to specified heirs
4. Not spoken
5. Arising from or contributing to the satisfaction of sensual desires
6. Sudden outburst of emotion or action
7. Unshakably calm and collected
11. Long, narrow opening; a crack or cleft
12. Causing annoyance, weariness, or vexation
13. Evade or escape from, as by daring, cleverness, or skill
14. Corrupt morally
16. Attack, as with ridicule
17. Disease, disorder, or ailment
18. Cite as an example or means of proof in an argument

Dracula Vocabulary Crossword 3

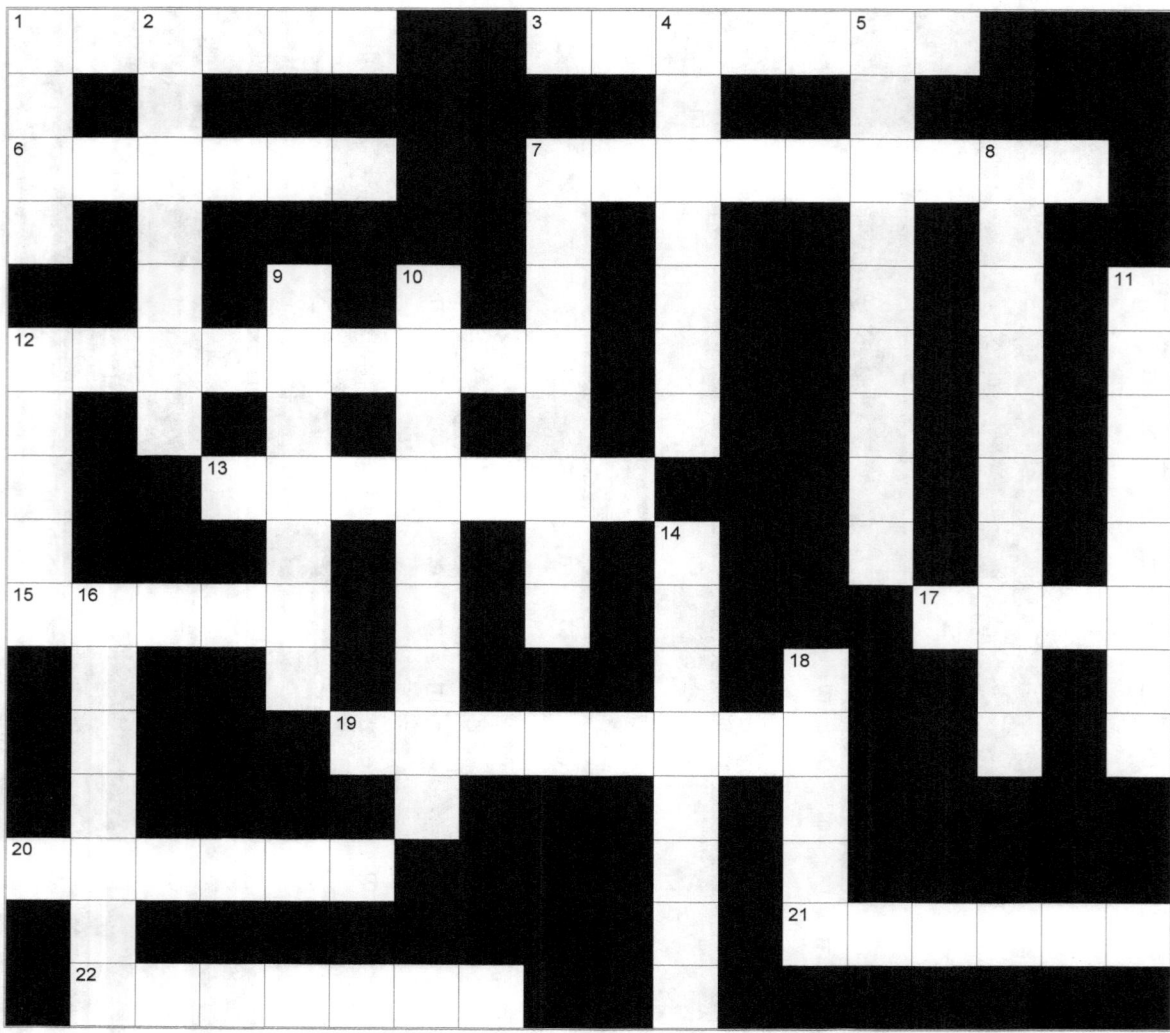

Across
1. Cite as an example or means of proof in an argument
3. Inflict grievous physical or mental suffering on
6. Polite, refined, and often elegant in manner
7. Practice of growing crops, & breeding and raising livestock
12. Yielded to an overwhelming desire; gave up or gave in
13. Matter-of-fact; straightforward; lacking imagination; dull
15. Evade or escape from, as by daring, cleverness, or skill
17. Marked by skill in deception
19. Limited inheritance of property to specified heirs
20. Agitation of the mind or emotions
21. Disease, disorder, or ailment
22. Separates or purifies

Down
1. Chill or fit of shivering
2. Corrupt morally
4. Long, narrow opening; a crack or cleft
5. Came together from different directions
7. Take in by deceptive means; deceive
8. Beginning again
9. Questioned; inquired
10. Low or downcast state
11. Sudden outburst of emotion or action
12. Struck down or hit
14. Producing abundant works or results
16. Lacking energy or vitality; weak
18. Strong dislike, contempt or aversion

Dracula Vocabulary Crossword 3 Answer Key

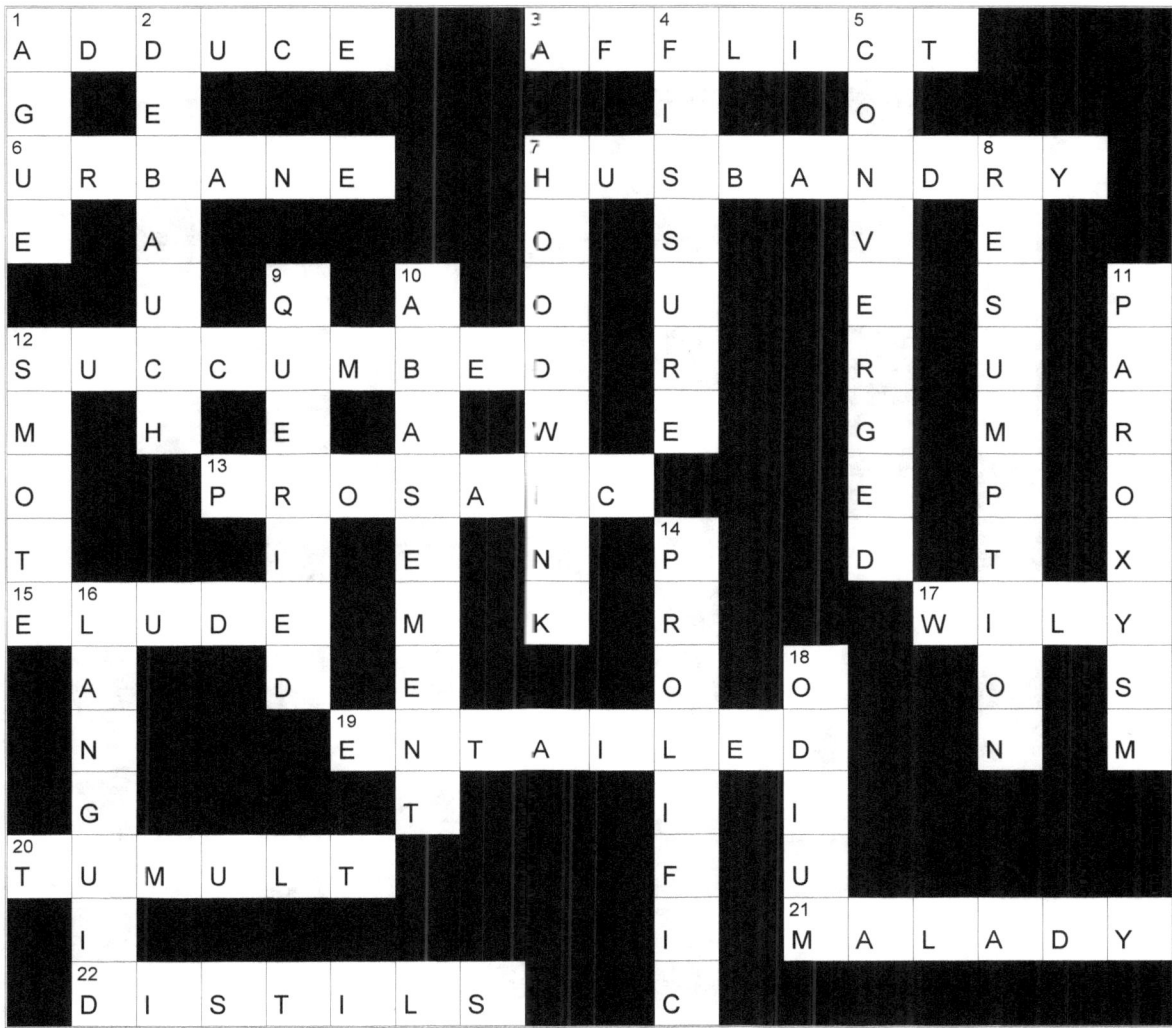

Across
1. Cite as an example or means of proof in an argument
3. Inflict grievous physical or mental suffering on
6. Polite, refined, and often elegant in manner
7. Practice of growing crops, & breeding and raising livestock
12. Yielded to an overwhelming desire; gave up or gave in
13. Matter-of-fact; straightforward; lacking imagination; dull
15. Evade or escape from, as by daring, cleverness, or skill
17. Marked by skill in deception
19. Limited inheritance of property to specified heirs
20. Agitation of the mind or emotions
21. Disease, disorder, or ailment
22. Separates or purifies

Down
1. Chill or fit of shivering
2. Corrupt morally
4. Long, narrow opening; a crack or cleft
5. Came together from different directions
7. Take in by deceptive means; deceive
8. Beginning again
9. Questioned; inquired
10. Low or downcast state
11. Sudden outburst of emotion or action
12. Struck down or hit
14. Producing abundant works or results
16. Lacking energy or vitality; weak
18. Strong dislike, contempt or aversion

Dracula Vocabulary Crossword 4

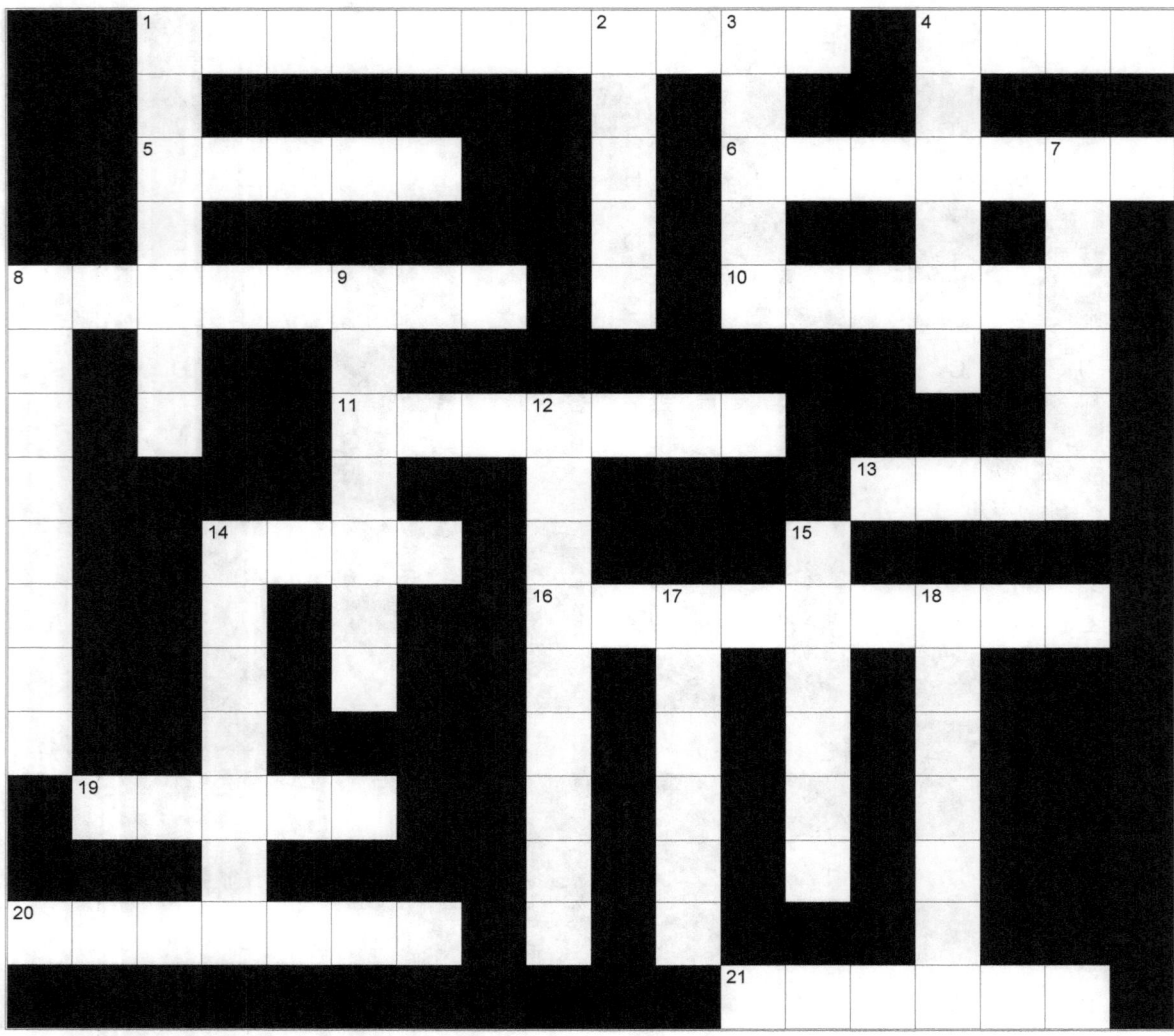

Across
1. One's usual mood; temperament
4. Chill or fit of shivering
5. Struck down or hit
6. Causing annoyance, weariness, or vexation
8. Distressing to the mind or feelings; profoundly moving or touching
10. Relating to work regarded as for a servant
11. Long, narrow opening; a crack or cleft
13. Marked by skill in deception
14. Den or dwelling of a wild animal; a hideaway
16. Practice of growing crops, & breeding and raising livestock
19. Evade or escape from, as by daring, cleverness, or skill
20. Relating to commonplace things; ordinary
21. Restrain for holding an animal in place

Down
1. Separates or purifies
2. Not spoken
3. Strong dislike, contempt or aversion
4. Attack, as with ridicule
7. Disease, disorder, or ailment
8. Sudden outburst of emotion or action
9. Inflict grievous physical or mental suffering on
12. Characteristic of a scholar or thinker
14. Lacking energy or vitality; weak
15. Extreme or unnatural paleness
17. Employee responsible for the upkeep of church property
18. Corrupt morally

Dracula Vocabulary Crossword 4 Answer Key

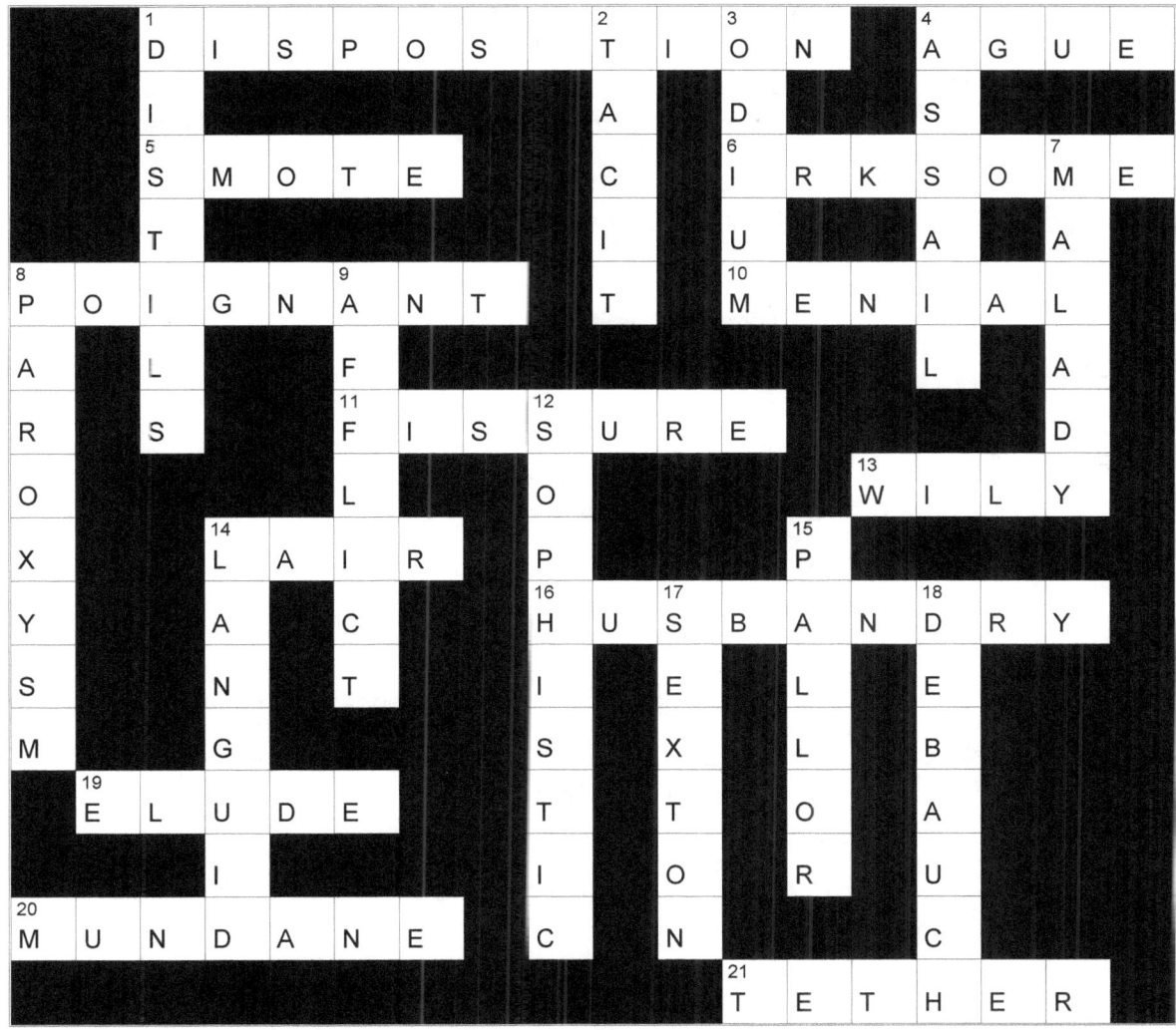

Across
1. One's usual mood; temperament
4. Chill or fit of shivering
5. Struck down or hit
6. Causing annoyance, weariness, or vexation
8. Distressing to the mind or feelings; profoundly moving or touching
10. Relating to work regarded as for a servant
11. Long, narrow opening; a crack or cleft
13. Marked by skill in deception
14. Den or dwelling of a wild animal; a hideaway
16. Practice of growing crops, & breeding and raising livestock
19. Evade or escape from, as by daring, cleverness, or skill
20. Relating to commonplace things; ordinary
21. Restrain for holding an animal in place

Down
1. Separates or purifies
2. Not spoken
3. Strong dislike, contempt or aversion
4. Attack, as with ridicule
7. Disease, disorder, or ailment
8. Sudden outburst of emotion or action
9. Inflict grievous physical or mental suffering on
12. Characteristic of a scholar or thinker
14. Lacking energy or vitality; weak
15. Extreme or unnatural paleness
17. Employee responsible for the upkeep of church property
18. Corrupt morally

Dracula Vocabulary Juggle Letters 1

1. NSIOMTAISAIL = 1. _____
   Adopting the customs and attitudes of the prevailing culture

2. TAAEDB = 2. _____
   Reduced in amount, degree, or intensity

3. WIDHOONK = 3. _____
   Take in by deceptive means; deceive

4. BUAREN = 4. _____
   Polite, refined, and often elegant in manner

5. NRLTYEEEVR = 5. _____
   In a state of profound awe and respect and often love

6. OTIUQIIISNN = 6. _____
   The act of inquiring into a matter; an investigation

7. DMADNUDE = 7. _____
   Something added or to be added, as in a supplement to a book

8. IINSOOITSPD = 8. _____
   One's usual mood; temperament

9. NGNAOTIP = 9. _____
   Distressing to the mind or feelings; profoundly moving or touching

10. IATARCLY = 10. _____
    Cheerful willingness; eagerness; speed or quickness

11. MANEEASBT = 11. _____
    Low or downcast state

12. AGTLEMICINA = 12. _____
    Puzzling or mysterious

13. ICMEENNE = 13. _____
    Position of great distinction or superiority

14. NEDEECREF = 14. _____
    Yielding to the opinion, wishes, or judgment of another

Dracula Vocabulary Juggle Letters 1 Answer Key

1. NSIOMTAISAIL = 1. ASSIMILATION
   Adopting the customs and attitudes of the prevailing culture

2. TAAEDB = 2. ABATED
   Reduced in amount, degree, or intensity

3. WIDHOONK = 3. HOODWINK
   Take in by deceptive means; deceive

4. BUAREN = 4. URBANE
   Polite, refined, and often elegant in manner

5. NRLTYEEEVR = 5. REVERENTLY
   In a state of profound awe and respect and often love

6. OTIUQIIISNN = 6. INQUISITION
   The act of inquiring into a matter; an investigation

7. DMADNUDE = 7. ADDENDUM
   Something added or to be added, as in a supplement to a book

8. IINSOOITSPD = 8. DISPOSITION
   One's usual mood; temperament

9. NGNAOTIP = 9. POIGNANT
   Distressing to the mind or feelings; profoundly moving or touching

10. IATARCLY =10. ALACRITY
    Cheerful willingness; eagerness; speed or quickness

11. MANEEASBT =11. ABASEMENT
    Low or downcast state

12. AGTLEMICINA =12. ENIGMATICAL
    Puzzling or mysterious

13. ICMEENNE =13. EMINENCE
    Position of great distinction or superiority

14. NEDEECREF =14. DEFERENCE
    Yielding to the opinion, wishes, or judgment of another

Dracula Vocabulary Juggle Letters 2

1. SUSAULDYOIS = 1. _____
   With care and persistence

2. NRREOTT = 2. _____
   Heavy, uncontrolled outpouring

3. GDUOIRPIOS = 3. _____
   Impressively great in size, force, or extent; enormous

4. ODRAIAM = 4. _____
   Scene in which figures are arranged in a naturalistic setting against a painted background

5. OTRNGAIGEMOLA = 5. _____
   Confused or jumbled mass

6. DBANHSRUY = 6. _____
   Practice of growing crops, & breeding and raising livestock

7. AMSTLEMRO = 7. _____
   Violent or turbulent situation; a large, violent whirlpool

8. YLCPTDIIA = 8. _____
   Quality of being undisturbed by tumult or disorder; relaxation

9. OARNETNS = 9. _____
   Strong and deep in tone

10. OIORDUB = 10. _____
    Woman's private sitting room, dressing room, or bedroom

11. EPDAISISDT = 11. _____
    Drove away; dispersed

12. CESAITARN = 12. _____
    Make certain, definite, and precise

13. SREMOKI = 13. _____
    Causing annoyance, weariness, or vexation

14. TIOIHSPCS = 14. _____
    Characteristic of a scholar or thinker

Dracula Vocabulary Juggle Letters 2 Answer Key

1. SUSAULDYOIS = 1. ASSIDUOUSLY
   With care and persistence

2. NRREOTT = 2. TORRENT
   Heavy, uncontrolled outpouring

3. GDUOIRPIOS = 3. PRODIGIOUS
   Impressively great in size, force, or extent; enormous

4. ODRAIAM = 4. DIORAMA
   Scene in which figures are arranged in a naturalistic setting against a painted background

5. OTRNGAIGEMOLA = 5. AGGLOMERATION
   Confused or jumbled mass

6. DBANHSRUY = 6. HUSBANDRY
   Practice of growing crops, & breeding and raising livestock

7. AMSTLEMRO = 7. MAELSTROM
   Violent or turbulent situation; a large, violent whirlpool

8. YLCPTDIIA = 8. PLACIDITY
   Quality of being undisturbed by tumult or disorder; relaxation

9. OARNETNS = 9. RESONANT
   Strong and deep in tone

10. OIORDUB = 10. BOUDOIR
    Woman's private sitting room, dressing room, or bedroom

11. EPDAISISDT = 11. DISSIPATED
    Drove away; dispersed

12. CESAITARN = 12. ASCERTAIN
    Make certain, definite, and precise

13. SREMOKI = 13. IRKSOME
    Causing annoyance, weariness, or vexation

14. TIOIHSPCS = 14. SOPHISTIC
    Characteristic of a scholar or thinker

Dracula Vocabulary Juggle Letters 3

1. IRGAHCN = 1. _____
   Strong feelings of embarrassment

2. TUUEIEDQIN = 2. _____
   State of restlessness or uneasiness

3. ETNDROISANC = 3. _____
   In a forced or inhibited manner

4. YROMPAXS = 4. _____
   Sudden outburst of emotion or action

5. UEIGNANS = 5. _____
   Cheerfully confident; optimistic; of a healthy reddish color

6. GRPODIUSIO = 6. _____
   Impressively great in size, force, or extent; enormous

7. AITTC = 7. _____
   Not spoken

8. DANUEMN = 8. _____
   Relating to commonplace things; ordinary

9. SCADTPHE = 9. _____
   Written, official message sent with speed

10. SGATINIINOT =10. _____
    Deliberate triggering of trouble or discord

11. SIPTOSCHI =11. _____
    Characteristic of a scholar or thinker

12. EDEREEFCN =12. _____
    Yielding to the opinion, wishes, or judgment of another

13. DUREATIPED =13. _____
    Rejected emphatically as unfounded, untrue, or unjust

14. EBNUAR =14. _____
    Polite, refined, and often elegant in manner

Dracula Vocabulary Juggle Letters 3 Answer Key

1. IRGAHCN = 1. CHAGRIN
Strong feelings of embarrassment

2. TUUEIEDQIN = 2. INQUIETUDE
State of restlessness or uneasiness

3. ETNDROISANC = 3. CONSTRAINED
In a forced or inhibited manner

4. YROMPAXS = 4. PAROXYSM
Sudden outburst of emotion or action

5. UEIGNANS = 5. SANGUINE
Cheerfully confident; optimistic; of a healthy reddish color

6. GRPODIUSIO = 6. PRODIGIOUS
Impressively great in size, force, or extent; enormous

7. AITTC = 7. TACIT
Not spoken

8. DANUEMN = 8. MUNDANE
Relating to commonplace things; ordinary

9. SCADTPHE = 9. DESPATCH
Written, official message sent with speed

10. SGATINIINOT = 10. INSTIGATION
Deliberate triggering of trouble or discord

11. SIPTOSCHI = 11. SOPHISTIC
Characteristic of a scholar or thinker

12. EDEREEFCN = 12. DEFERENCE
Yielding to the opinion, wishes, or judgment of another

13. DUREATIPED = 13. REPUDIATED
Rejected emphatically as unfounded, untrue, or unjust

14. EBNUAR = 14. URBANE
Polite, refined, and often elegant in manner

Dracula Vocabulary Juggle Letters 4

1. ISILSDT = 1. _____
Separates or purifies

2. DEENILAT = 2. _____
Limited inheritance of property to specified heirs

3. INSOTSIRUEQI = 3. _____
Formal, written requests for something needed

4. ICDSEEQCAU = 4. _____
Consent or comply passively or without protest

5. VARITMEB = 5. _____
In exactly the same words; word for word

6. ENOCGVEDR = 6. _____
Came together from different directions

7. SBDYHNRAU = 7. _____
Practice of growing crops, & breeding and raising livestock

8. ENRDEEECF = 8. _____
Yielding to the opinion, wishes, or judgment of another

9. ERCASTNAI = 9. _____
Make certain, definite, and precise

10. RLIA = 10. _____
Den or dwelling of a wild animal; a hideaway

11. ILWY = 11. _____
Marked by skill in deception

12. ETTICREN = 12. _____
Inclined to keep one's thoughts, feelings, and personal affairs to oneself

13. SPSHOICIT = 13. _____
Characteristic of a scholar or thinker

14. AAECUDNTTCE = 14. _____
Stressed or emphasized; intensified

Dracula Vocabulary Juggle Letters 4 Answer Key

1. ISILSDT = 1. DISTILS
   Separates or purifies

2. DEENILAT = 2. ENTAILED
   Limited inheritance of property to specified heirs

3. INSOTSIRUEQI = 3. REQUISITIONS
   Formal, written requests for something needed

4. ICDSEEQCAU = 4. ACQUIESCED
   Consent or comply passively or without protest

5. VARITMEB = 5. VERBATIM
   In exactly the same words; word for word

6. ENOCGVEDR = 6. CONVERGED
   Came together from different directions

7. SBDYHNRAU = 7. HUSBANDRY
   Practice of growing crops, & breeding and raising livestock

8. ENRDEEECF = 8. DEFERENCE
   Yielding to the opinion, wishes, or judgment of another

9. ERCASTNAI = 9. ASCERTAIN
   Make certain, definite, and precise

10. RLIA = 10. LAIR
    Den or dwelling of a wild animal; a hideaway

11. ILWY = 11. WILY
    Marked by skill in deception

12. ETTICREN = 12. RETICENT
    Inclined to keep one's thoughts, feelings, and personal affairs to oneself

13. SPSHOICIT = 13. SOPHISTIC
    Characteristic of a scholar or thinker

14. AAECUDNTTCE = 14. ACCENTUATED
    Stressed or emphasized; intensified

ABASEMENT	Low or downcast state
ABATED	Reduced in amount, degree, or intensity
ACCENTUATED	Stressed or emphasized; intensified
ACQUIESCED	Consented or complied passively or without protest
ACQUIESCED	Consent or comply passively or without protest

ACUMEN	Quickness, accuracy, and keenness of judgment or insight
ADDENDUM	Something added or to be added, as in a supplement to a book
ADDUCE	Cite as an example or means of proof in an argument
AFFLICT	Inflict grievous physical or mental suffering on
AGGLOMERATION	Confused or jumbled mass

AGUE	Chill or fit of shivering
ALACRITY	Cheerful willingness; eagerness; speed or quickness
AMENABLE	Responsive to advice, authority, or suggestion; willing
ASCERTAIN	Make certain, definite, and precise
ASSAIL	Attack, as with ridicule

ASSIDUOUSLY	With care and persistence
ASSIMILATION	Adopting the customs and attitudes of the prevailing culture
AVARICE	Immoderate desire for wealth; greed
BOUDOIR	Woman's private sitting room, dressing room, or bedroom
CALECHE	Light carriage with two or four low wheels and a collapsible top

CHAGRIN	Strong feelings of embarrassment
CONSIGNING	Giving over to the care of another
CONSTRAINED	In a forced or inhibited manner
CONVERGED	Came together from different directions
DEBAUCH	Corrupt morally

DEFERENCE	Yielding to the opinion, wishes, or judgment of another
DEMURRED	Voiced opposition; objected
DESPATCH	Written, official message sent with speed
DIORAMA	Scene in which figures are arranged in a naturalistic setting against a painted background
DISPOSITION	One's usual mood; temperament

DISSIPATED	Drove away; dispersed
DISTILS	Separates or purifies
ELUDE	Evade or escape from, as by daring, cleverness, or skill
EMACIATED	Extremely thin, especially as a result of starvation
EMINENCE	Position of great distinction or superiority

ENIGMATICAL	Puzzling or mysterious
ENTAILED	Limited inheritance of property to specified heirs
EXPOSTULATE	Reason with someone in an effort to dissuade or correct
FISSURE	Long, narrow opening; a crack or cleft
HAGGARD	Appearing worn and exhausted

HOODWINK	Take in by deceptive means; deceive
HUSBANDRY	Practice of growing crops, & breeding and raising livestock
IMPERTURBABLE	Unshakably calm and collected
IMPLICITLY	In a manner which is understood though not directly expressed
IMPOTENT	Lacking physical strength or vigor; weak

IMPREGNABLE	Impossible to capture or enter by force
INQUIETUDE	State of restlessness or uneasiness
INQUISITION	The act of inquiring into a matter; an investigation
INSTIGATION	Deliberate triggering of trouble or discord
INTRIGUED	Engaged in secret or underhanded schemes; spied

IRKSOME	Causing annoyance, weariness, or vexation
LAIR	Den or dwelling of a wild animal; a hideaway
LANGUID	Lacking energy or vitality; weak
MAELSTROM	Violent or turbulent situation; a large, violent whirlpool
MALADY	Disease, disorder, or ailment

MALIGNITY	Intense ill will or hatred; great malice
MALODOROUS	Having a bad odor; foul
MENIAL	Relating to work regarded as for a servant
MUNDANE	Relating to commonplace things; ordinary
ODIUM	Strong dislike, contempt or aversion

PALLOR	Extreme or unnatural paleness
PAROXYSM	Sudden outburst of emotion or action
PLACIDITY	Quality of being undisturbed by tumult or disorder; relaxation
POIGNANT	Distressing to the mind or feelings; profoundly moving or touching
PORTERAGE	Charge for the carrying of burdens or goods as done by porters

PRESAGE	Indication or warning of a future occurrence; an omen
PRODIGIOUS	Impressively great in size, force, or extent; enormous
PROLIFIC	Producing abundant works or results
PROSAIC	Matter-of-fact; straightforward; lacking imagination; dull
QUERIED	Questioned; inquired

REMONSTRANCE	Expression of protest or complaint
REPUDIATED	Rejected emphatically as unfounded, untrue, or unjust
REQUISITIONS	Formal, written requests for something needed
RESONANT	Strong and deep in tone
RESUMPTION	Beginning again

RETICENT	Inclined to keep one's thoughts, feelings, and personal affairs to oneself
REVERENTLY	In a state of profound awe and respect and often love
SANGUINE	Cheerfully confident; optimistic; of a healthy reddish color
SATURNINE	Melancholy or sullen; tending to be bitter
SEXTON	Employee responsible for the upkeep of church property

SMOTE	Struck down or hit
SOPHISTIC	Characteristic of a scholar or thinker
STALWART	Having or marked by imposing physical strength
SUCCUMBED	Yielded to an overwhelming desire; gave up or gave in
TACIT	Not spoken

TETHER	Restrain for holding an animal in place
THWARTING	Opposing and defeating the efforts, plans, or ambitions of something
TORRENT	Heavy, uncontrolled outpouring
TRENCHANT	Forceful, effective, and vigorous
TUMULT	Agitation of the mind or emotions

UNFETTERED	Set free or kept free from restrictions or bonds
UNHALLOWED	Unholy
URBANE	Polite, refined, and often elegant in manner
VERBATIM	In exactly the same words; word for word
VIADUCT	Bridge consisting of arches used to carry a road over a valley

VOLUPTUOUS	Arising from or contributing to the satisfaction of sensual desires
WILY	Marked by skill in deception

Dracula Vocabulary

LAIR	SUCCUMBED	PAROXYSM	DEMURRED	TUMULT
PROSAIC	HUSBANDRY	RESUMPTION	REPUDIATED	ACQUIESCED
ASSIDUOUSLY	ENIGMATICAL	FREE SPACE	HAGGARD	ASSIMILATION
UNHALLOWED	HOODWINK	MALODOROUS	AGUE	EXPOSTULATE
AFFLICT	INQUISITION	PLACIDITY	VOLUPTUOUS	PRODIGIOUS

Dracula Vocabulary

ENTAILED	DESPATCH	RETICENT	TACIT	BOUDOIR
URBANE	RESONANT	ASCERTAIN	TRENCHANT	ACCENTUATED
ABATED	INQUIETUDE	FREE SPACE	ADDENDUM	TETHER
PORTERAGE	CALECHE	CONSTRAINED	ACUMEN	SATURNINE
INTRIGUED	EMINENCE	THWARTING	STALWART	UNFETTERED

Dracula Vocabulary

INTRIGUED	SATURNINE	SANGUINE	TETHER	ALACRITY
DESPATCH	ASSAIL	ACCENTUATED	IMPLICITLY	DIORAMA
EMACIATED	PRODIGIOUS	FREE SPACE	SEXTON	LAIR
SOPHISTIC	HOODWINK	ELUDE	BOUDOIR	SMOTE
IRKSOME	ACQUIESCED	ENIGMATICAL	IMPREGNABLE	ABASEMENT

Dracula Vocabulary

ACUMEN	VOLUPTUOUS	LANGUID	CONSIGNING	ADDUCE
ODIUM	DEMURRED	PROLIFIC	INQUISITION	INQUIETUDE
REMONSTRANCE	UNHALLOWED	FREE SPACE	EMINENCE	MAELSTROM
DEFERENCE	ACQUIESCED	MALODOROUS	MUNDANE	RESUMPTION
VERBATIM	HAGGARD	TORRENT	CHAGRIN	CALECHE

Dracula Vocabulary

MENIAL	INTRIGUED	PORTERAGE	QUERIED	AGGLOMERATION
VIADUCT	ASSIDUOUSLY	IMPERTURBABLE	VERBATIM	HOODWINK
PROSAIC	ENIGMATICAL	FREE SPACE	MALADY	SEXTON
EMACIATED	DEMURRED	PROLIFIC	REVERENTLY	SATURNINE
ENTAILED	ADDENDUM	PAROXYSM	AGUE	AMENABLE

Dracula Vocabulary

TORRENT	DEBAUCH	ABATED	REQUISITIONS	MUNDANE
ACUMEN	HUSBANDRY	AFFLICT	UNHALLOWED	ACQUIESCED
CHAGRIN	ODIUM	FREE SPACE	ELUDE	PRODIGIOUS
CONSTRAINED	SOPHISTIC	STALWART	THWARTING	ABASEMENT
VOLUPTUOUS	REMONSTRANCE	LAIR	SUCCUMBED	INQUIETUDE

Dracula Vocabulary

TETHER	VERBATIM	EMINENCE	IMPREGNABLE	ASCERTAIN
PLACIDITY	PRODIGIOUS	CONVERGED	VIADUCT	CONSIGNING
RETICENT	BOUDOIR	FREE SPACE	LANGUID	ASSAIL
IRKSOME	ADDUCE	DEFERENCE	HUSBANDRY	ABASEMENT
MALIGNITY	UNHALLOWED	SMOTE	EMACIATED	ACUMEN

Dracula Vocabulary

WILY	REQUISITIONS	VOLUPTUOUS	DIORAMA	ASSIMILATION
ASSIDUOUSLY	SEXTON	PROSAIC	IMPERTURBABLE	DISPOSITION
TUMULT	ABATED	FREE SPACE	AVARICE	IMPOTENT
REPUDIATED	AGUE	AGGLOMERATION	LAIR	DISTILS
MAELSTROM	ODIUM	ACQUIESCED	SANGUINE	ELUDE

Dracula Vocabulary

MALODOROUS	ASSIDUOUSLY	SMOTE	VOLUPTUOUS	TUMULT
EMACIATED	CONSTRAINED	UNHALLOWED	RESUMPTION	TRENCHANT
THWARTING	HOODWINK	FREE SPACE	ALACRITY	REPUDIATED
ABATED	ABASEMENT	EMINENCE	PORTERAGE	SOPHISTIC
ACCENTUATED	CONSIGNING	CONVERGED	ASCERTAIN	AGGLOMERATION

Dracula Vocabulary

SEXTON	ACQUIESCED	IMPLICITLY	INTRIGUED	POIGNANT
PALLOR	VIADUCT	DESPATCH	IMPREGNABLE	LANGUID
INQUIETUDE	TETHER	FREE SPACE	WILY	REVERENTLY
DEFERENCE	DEMURRED	ACQUIESCED	STALWART	URBANE
IRKSOME	ASSAIL	MENIAL	INSTIGATION	REMONSTRANCE

Dracula Vocabulary

CALECHE	ADDENDUM	SUCCUMBED	ASSAIL	REPUDIATED
RESUMPTION	BOUDOIR	MUNDANE	ENIGMATICAL	AVARICE
CONVERGED	REVERENTLY	FREE SPACE	IMPERTURBABLE	URBANE
SANGUINE	TRENCHANT	PROSAIC	DESPATCH	ASSIDUOUSLY
SEXTON	PAROXYSM	DISTILS	INQUISITION	INSTIGATION

Dracula Vocabulary

EMACIATED	DISSIPATED	MAELSTROM	DEBAUCH	ACQUIESCED
INTRIGUED	DIORAMA	POIGNANT	MALIGNITY	DEMURRED
PORTERAGE	PROLIFIC	FREE SPACE	HOODWINK	VERBATIM
WILY	VIADUCT	PRESAGE	ASCERTAIN	AMENABLE
DEFERENCE	QUERIED	HUSBANDRY	ASSIMILATION	ALACRITY

Dracula Vocabulary

RESONANT	VERBATIM	IMPREGNABLE	ODIUM	ELUDE
THWARTING	MAELSTROM	DISSIPATED	SMOTE	AGUE
ASCERTAIN	LANGUID	FREE SPACE	TUMULT	LAIR
MUNDANE	ENTAILED	REQUISITIONS	PALLOR	CALECHE
IMPOTENT	SEXTON	AMENABLE	EMACIATED	EXPOSTULATE

Dracula Vocabulary

ACUMEN	TETHER	SUCCUMBED	AVARICE	TACIT
MALIGNITY	PROLIFIC	HUSBANDRY	CHAGRIN	SOPHISTIC
ABASEMENT	CONSTRAINED	FREE SPACE	VOLUPTUOUS	ABATED
ADDUCE	DISTILS	POIGNANT	REMONSTRANCE	MALODOROUS
DESPATCH	UNFETTERED	MENIAL	PRODIGIOUS	AGGLOMERATION

Dracula Vocabulary

TORRENT	HOODWINK	TACIT	IMPERTURBABLE	MENIAL
ABASEMENT	BOUDOIR	PALLOR	CHAGRIN	REQUISITIONS
MALADY	INSTIGATION	FREE SPACE	VIADUCT	FISSURE
EMACIATED	ASCERTAIN	AGGLOMERATION	ENTAILED	REMONSTRANCE
ELUDE	ACCENTUATED	AGUE	IMPOTENT	SANGUINE

Dracula Vocabulary

DIORAMA	DISTILS	TRENCHANT	DISSIPATED	ACQUIESCED
UNHALLOWED	IMPLICITLY	DEMURRED	IRKSOME	DESPATCH
TETHER	STALWART	FREE SPACE	MALIGNITY	PROSAIC
SEXTON	URBANE	PORTERAGE	PROLIFIC	ASSAIL
RETICENT	ALACRITY	PRODIGIOUS	POIGNANT	MUNDANE

Dracula Vocabulary

MENIAL	ACCENTUATED	ODIUM	LAIR	DIORAMA
IRKSOME	INQUISITION	ENTAILED	IMPREGNABLE	AFFLICT
ASSAIL	REPUDIATED	FREE SPACE	SANGUINE	CONVERGED
TRENCHANT	LANGUID	ADDUCE	EXPOSTULATE	CONSTRAINED
RESUMPTION	ACUMEN	REVERENTLY	ASCERTAIN	INTRIGUED

Dracula Vocabulary

UNFETTERED	UNHALLOWED	BOUDOIR	AMENABLE	INQUIETUDE
ACQUIESCED	SATURNINE	URBANE	TACIT	IMPLICITLY
PROSAIC	PALLOR	FREE SPACE	ABATED	DEBAUCH
MALODOROUS	PAROXYSM	CALECHE	REMONSTRANCE	THWARTING
PRODIGIOUS	POIGNANT	DEFERENCE	MUNDANE	ASSIDUOUSLY

Dracula Vocabulary

MALODOROUS	ENTAILED	IMPOTENT	DEBAUCH	LANGUID
DESPATCH	VIADUCT	SANGUINE	HAGGARD	PRESAGE
PALLOR	ELUDE	FREE SPACE	TACIT	TRENCHANT
STALWART	TORRENT	HOODWINK	ACQUIESCED	VERBATIM
DEMURRED	DISTILS	CONVERGED	QUERIED	EMINENCE

Dracula Vocabulary

INTRIGUED	AFFLICT	PROLIFIC	IMPERTURBABLE	DEFERENCE
ASSAIL	ALACRITY	CHAGRIN	ACCENTUATED	AVARICE
MENIAL	INQUIETUDE	FREE SPACE	AGUE	UNFETTERED
ASSIMILATION	IMPLICITLY	RESUMPTION	MUNDANE	PORTERAGE
ADDENDUM	SEXTON	ABASEMENT	REPUDIATED	CALECHE

Dracula Vocabulary

INQUIETUDE	SEXTON	DEFERENCE	MAELSTROM	ENIGMATICAL
PROSAIC	LANGUID	IMPREGNABLE	ADDUCE	CONSIGNING
HOODWINK	TRENCHANT	FREE SPACE	DEMURRED	QUERIED
THWARTING	PLACIDITY	PAROXYSM	RETICENT	REPUDIATED
ASSIDUOUSLY	UNHALLOWED	MENIAL	RESONANT	AVARICE

Dracula Vocabulary

IRKSOME	DIORAMA	ACUMEN	ODIUM	BOUDOIR
TUMULT	SMOTE	EMINENCE	UNFETTERED	URBANE
ACCENTUATED	INSTIGATION	FREE SPACE	ABATED	ABASEMENT
MALODOROUS	CONVERGED	TACIT	PRODIGIOUS	RESUMPTION
AFFLICT	AGUE	VIADUCT	IMPLICITLY	CALECHE

Dracula Vocabulary

PAROXYSM	TACIT	DEFERENCE	AGGLOMERATION	DESPATCH
ENIGMATICAL	REQUISITIONS	HAGGARD	SANGUINE	DISTILS
ADDENDUM	PROSAIC	FREE SPACE	VIADUCT	QUERIED
CHAGRIN	PALLOR	RETICENT	ADDUCE	FISSURE
PORTERAGE	MALIGNITY	REVERENTLY	ACQUIESCED	BOUDOIR

Dracula Vocabulary

ASSIMILATION	EXPOSTULATE	MUNDANE	IRKSOME	REPUDIATED
SATURNINE	TUMULT	POIGNANT	INQUIETUDE	AFFLICT
REMONSTRANCE	ODIUM	FREE SPACE	RESONANT	ASSAIL
CONVERGED	INTRIGUED	SUCCUMBED	ACQUIESCED	EMACIATED
TORRENT	MAELSTROM	DEBAUCH	MALADY	URBANE

Dracula Vocabulary

IMPERTURBABLE	ABASEMENT	DIORAMA	UNFETTERED	ELUDE
DEFERENCE	DESPATCH	REMONSTRANCE	LANGUID	IMPREGNABLE
IMPOTENT	RESONANT	FREE SPACE	BOUDOIR	EMACIATED
VIADUCT	ASCERTAIN	EXPOSTULATE	DEMURRED	TORRENT
MALIGNITY	CONVERGED	REVERENTLY	THWARTING	PORTERAGE

Dracula Vocabulary

PALLOR	AGUE	ABATED	HUSBANDRY	ALACRITY
ASSIMILATION	QUERIED	MENIAL	ADDENDUM	PRODIGIOUS
REQUISITIONS	VERBATIM	FREE SPACE	SOPHISTIC	ENTAILED
SEXTON	INTRIGUED	POIGNANT	MUNDANE	RETICENT
SUCCUMBED	CHAGRIN	ENIGMATICAL	MALADY	REPUDIATED

Dracula Vocabulary

TETHER	SATURNINE	CALECHE	SMOTE	CONVERGED
HUSBANDRY	IMPLICITLY	ASSIDUOUSLY	IMPERTURBABLE	INTRIGUED
ABATED	RESUMPTION	FREE SPACE	QUERIED	AFFLICT
AVARICE	PORTERAGE	LAIR	ADDENDUM	TUMULT
VIADUCT	FISSURE	ADDUCE	CONSTRAINED	MALADY

Dracula Vocabulary

VOLUPTUOUS	ELUDE	PRESAGE	PROLIFIC	UNHALLOWED
DEMURRED	MALODOROUS	ACUMEN	TORRENT	POIGNANT
DISPOSITION	BOUDOIR	FREE SPACE	REMONSTRANCE	SOPHISTIC
PROSAIC	ENTAILED	IRKSOME	URBANE	MALIGNITY
HOODWINK	AMENABLE	LANGUID	CONSIGNING	EMINENCE

Dracula Vocabulary

REMONSTRANCE	MALIGNITY	EMACIATED	AFFLICT	ASSIMILATION
AGUE	INQUIETUDE	ACUMEN	ODIUM	DIORAMA
VERBATIM	EXPOSTULATE	FREE SPACE	CALECHE	ACQUIESCED
IMPREGNABLE	RESONANT	HUSBANDRY	URBANE	AVARICE
PAROXYSM	PLACIDITY	INTRIGUED	INSTIGATION	LANGUID

Dracula Vocabulary

CONVERGED	ASSIDUOUSLY	SATURNINE	ACCENTUATED	ASSAIL
QUERIED	ACQUIESCED	DESPATCH	DISPOSITION	RESUMPTION
ABASEMENT	ENIGMATICAL	FREE SPACE	PRODIGIOUS	SEXTON
TACIT	FISSURE	SOPHISTIC	DEBAUCH	ENTAILED
DISTILS	WILY	DEMURRED	DEFERENCE	PORTERAGE

Dracula Vocabulary

LANGUID	REPUDIATED	AVARICE	SANGUINE	IMPLICITLY
IMPREGNABLE	CHAGRIN	ACQUIESCED	TRENCHANT	HAGGARD
CONSTRAINED	ASSAIL	FREE SPACE	INSTIGATION	HUSBANDRY
ADDUCE	VOLUPTUOUS	REQUISITIONS	MENIAL	ALACRITY
EMINENCE	PROSAIC	DEFERENCE	ELUDE	AGUE

Dracula Vocabulary

DISSIPATED	TETHER	SEXTON	SATURNINE	URBANE
SMOTE	SUCCUMBED	DIORAMA	POIGNANT	IMPOTENT
DISTILS	RESONANT	FREE SPACE	CONVERGED	DEMURRED
EXPOSTULATE	WILY	AGGLOMERATION	MAELSTROM	IMPERTURBABLE
ODIUM	ENTAILED	PORTERAGE	MALADY	UNFETTERED